The Essential Guide to Life
After Bereavement

of related interest

How to Break Bad News to People with Intellectual Disabilities
A Guide for Carers and Professionals
Irene Tuffrey-Wijne
Foreword by Professor Baroness Sheila Hollins
ISBN 978 1 84905 280 1
eISBN 978 0 85700 583 0

After the Suicide
Helping the Bereaved to Find a Path from Grief to Recovery
Kari Dyregrov, Einar Plyhn and Gudrun Dieserud
Foreword by John R. Jordan
ISBN 978 1 84905 211 5
eISBN 978 0 85700 445 1

Communicating with Children When a Parent is at the End of Life
Rachel Fearnley
ISBN 978 1 84905 234 4
eISBN 978 0 85700 475 8

What Does Dead Mean?
A Book for Young Children to Help Explain Death and Dying
Caroline Jay and Jenni Thomas
Illustrated by Unity-Joy Dale
ISBN 978 1 84905 355 6
eISBN 978 0 85700 705 6

Children Also Grieve
Talking about Death and Healing
Linda Goldman
ISBN 978 1 84310 808 5
eISBN 978 1 84642 471 7

Great Answers to Difficult Questions about Death
What Children Need to Know
Linda Goldman
ISBN 978 1 84905 805 6
eISBN 978 1 84642 957 6

The Essential Guide to

LIFE *After*
BEREAVEMENT

Beyond Tomorrow

Judy Carole Kauffmann *and* Mary Jordan

FOREWORD BY CIARÁN DEVANE

Jessica Kingsley *Publishers*
London and Philadelphia

155.
937.

First published in 2013
by Jessica Kingsley Publishers
73 Collier Street
London N1 9BE, UK
and
400 Market Street, Suite 400
Philadelphia, PA 19106, USA

www.jkp.com

Library of Congress Cataloging in Publication Data
Carole Kauffmann, Judy.
   The essential guide to life after bereavement : beyond tomorrow / Judy Carole
Kauffmann and Mary Jordan ; foreword by Ciaran Devane.
      pages cm
   Includes bibliographical references and index.
   ISBN 978-1-84905-335-8 (alk. paper)
   1. Bereavement. 2. Loss (Psychology) 3. Death. I. Jordan, Mary, 1951- II. Title.
   BF575.G7C375 2013
   155.9'37--dc23
                        2013005838

British Library Cataloguing in Publication Data
A CIP catalogue record for this book is available from the British Library

ISBN 978 1 84905 335 8
eISBN 978 0 85700 669 1

Printed and bound in Great Britain

Contents

Foreword

Bereavement is one of the most common of human experiences. But surprisingly for such a common experience, it is often unnecessarily traumatic. The loss of a close relative or friend will never be less than painful. Perhaps it should never be less than painful. However, the short- and long-term trauma which we see so regularly is often beyond what is acceptable.

Over a hundred years ago a young civil servant founded what is now Macmillan Cancer Support. He did so because of the trauma he himself suffered when his father died of cancer. A hundred years ago a death from cancer was often painful and undignified – a 'bad' death. The young Douglas Macmillan set up the charity to help people with cancer to die well.

Sudden death, by trauma or a catastrophic health episode, can be the hardest of all. The shock, the lack of time to prepare, the practical and emotional crises they cause must be amongst the most difficult to dealt with. Helping in that situation is all the more critical.

However, most deaths are less sudden. There is time for individuals to plan, for their friends and family to prepare and for the services supporting them to put the right measures in place. And that is the first lesson in managing bereavement. It is so much easier if the death itself is calm and pain free. Helping people to have a good death, ideally at the place of their choosing, has to be a priority for those of us working in the field.

It goes without saying that support should not be withdrawn the instant someone dies. The feeling of abandonment when everyone packs up, goes home or moves on is acute. A carer who has invested so much for someone they love is never more alone than at that point.

Organizations such as Macmillan and Cruse Bereavement Care do provide bereavement support through our professionals and our support line. While we provide this to many thousands of people, we know there are many more who we do not reach. One of our challenges is to let people know we are there, in person, on the Macmillan Support Line, on our online community. But of course we also seek to help people help themselves by providing information to help people help themselves and help others.

Which is also where *The Essential Guide to Life After Bereavement: Beyond Tomorrow* comes in. Many of the things which cause problems on bereavement are common and can benefit from the lessons and experience of others. How to deal with personal effects, how to cope with the poor behaviour of others, how to talk about the death. All are things which many have experienced and often people have developed insight which has helped them and which they are happy to share.

My own example is from when Katy, my wife, died. The most useful advice was from my mother who advised me to 'get the firsts over with'. Some firsts look after themselves. The first birthday, the first Christmas, the first wedding anniversary. Others do not. The first visit to the favourite restaurant, the first holiday, the first time to meet some friends. My mother's advice was to get them out of the way on the sensible basis that second time is easier and putting things off only makes them more frightening.

Such practical but insightful advice is the basis of this book. It is written from experience and from listening to others. Whatever your role and whatever loss you are experiencing, I hope there is something in it which makes things that bit less painful, that bit sooner. Please read it and take from it what is helpful to you – and know there are many of us out there who did bounce back and who wish the same for you.

Ciarán Devane
Chief Executive
Macmillan Cancer Support

Acknowledgements

The case stories in this book have come from many sources and not everyone wished to have their names mentioned. We would like to thank all those who have generously shared their stories and their areas of expertise with us. They have no idea how much it is appreciated.

We would like to thank: Faith Warn, Alex Carpenter, Jeremy Ornellas, Geraldine White, Vikki Allport de Orbe, Bobbie Sylvestre, Joan Hughes, Nancy Bank, the inspirational managers from Inglewood Liz Hayes and Becky Morris, April Olins, Diane Hardiman, Dr. Shirley Holton, Ori Kauffmann, Patricia Palmer, Christine Parsons, Bernadette Losasso, Peter Palmer, Rauf and Tristram Jordan and Erica Arnold, our family and friends who gave us love and support and of course Ciaran Devane who wrote our foreword.

Our thanks must also go to Rachel Menzies our editor for her help and advice.

Introduction

When someone dies, our lives can change in the blink of an eye, and we are given no rehearsal time for the new roles we have to adopt. The stage-set design of our life changes as the old familiar scenery is swept away and an unfamiliar landscape takes its place. Our roles can change from wife to widow, from daughter to orphan, from brother to only living child. With an unfamiliar and seemingly desolate landscape ahead of us we may well find ourselves wondering how we will able to get beyond tomorrow.

Along with all the practical tasks we have to face comes the numbing and overwhelming ache that never seems to leave our side. Whilst trying to cope with the grief we can feel pulled in a hundred different directions knowing there are so many practical things that need to be done: people that need to be told, a funeral that needs to be arranged, paperwork that needs to be sorted through and possessions that need to be disposed of. The extended family, who may rarely meet, may find themselves thrown together for long periods with tension running high. Emotions bubble to the surface and old wounds may reopen. We may have to support others through their grief at a time when we are barely able to support ourselves. Painful and private anniversaries loom ahead – and all of this happens at a time when we are least able to cope with it.

Some friends seem to rise to the occasion whereas others cross the road to avoid us, not knowing what to say and perhaps believing that saying nothing is a preferable option to saying the wrong thing. This leaves us feeling alone and isolated exactly at a time when we most need to be comforted and to feel that others care.

No matter how prepared you think you will be, or think that you are, when someone dies you may find that logic and emotion are not always the best bedfellows. This book is a follow-up to our award-winning book *End of Life: The Essential Guide to Caring*, and it is written for anyone who needs an emotional 'satellite navigation' tool to guide them through the new landscape that has opened up without warning in front of them.

Breaking bad news

We may find ourselves having to break bad news about people we love, to people we love, and with no script to guide us. We perhaps imagine that we are unlikely to have that task, that this will be done by trained medical staff or the police, but breaking the news of a death to those nearest to the deceased is only part of the story. Even if a professional person such as a police officer or a doctor has told the next of kin then there will be others both within the family and beyond the family who need to be told.

All bad news, especially bad news that comes completely out of the blue, needs to be conveyed with care, and when we ourselves have been the recipient of the news and now have to pass it on to others, it is a very traumatic and unwelcome task.

This undertaking is made all the more complicated if there are children or people with intellectual disabilities or dementia who need to be told the news. What do we say? How do we say it? We want to soften the blow, to tell them in the 'right way', but what is the 'right way'? Is it really important for people with dementia to be told of the death? Will people with dementia remember what we said? Will they not forget that they have heard the news after a few moments so that we have to repeat it over and over again with the added factor of our own distress? And what about someone with an intellectual disability – do they have any concept of death? How can we explain death to them?

There are no books that give us any guidance on breaking bad news to people with dementia, and clearly there is no 'one size fits all' in any group, but the value of guidance and support through that minefield cannot be overestimated. News which is badly broken to others can add to the impact of the devastation for everyone.

Our knowledge and understanding of the long-term effects of excluding children from many aspects of terminal illness and death are now well-documented, but should children go to funerals? Is that too traumatic for them or is it important for them to be included there as well? Is it wise for people with dementia to be invited, and what about those with an intellectual disability? Should they be invited to attend a funeral or is it better for them not to go?

Grief

Having broken the bad news we then have to manoeuvre through that dark tunnel of our own grief. Grief is potentially the worst emotional pain any of us will suffer. In our chapter, More About Grief, we will tell you a bit about the theories that have been advanced about the passage of grief but also some of the facts. We will give some common-sense landmarks that we hope will take you through your grief, as well as some practical hints about how to get back into life again.

Attitudes concerning conversations around death seem still to be in the dark ages and, perversely, other people's well-intentioned comments or lack of comments can make grieving harder. What do you say when you don't know what to say?

Grief has a start date but no end date. There are theories about the 'stages of grief' that people pass through whilst mourning, but knowing the theories doesn't seem to help you in your grieving. When you experience a significant loss the grief can be a process that goes on for many years and it changes shape according to the stages of our life in which that person is missed. Nor does grief take a different route just because someone deteriorated over a long period before death, either physically or mentally or both. The role of being a carer can take over your life and when there is no longer someone to care for the gap that is left can feel like a huge crater. There can be a massive sense of 'nothingness'.

Guilt and grief

This book will address the issue of the guilty feelings that arise after death and discuss the demands made upon you by family and friends at this time. Guilt and grief seem to go hand-in-hand and as Elizabeth Kübler-Ross said, 'guilt is perhaps the most painful companion of death' (1969, p.169). Guilt has a habit of tapping on our shoulder in the early hours before dawn and no matter how illogical the guilty feeling may be, it is hard to shake it off. The finality of death seems to take us all by surprise. It can be really difficult just to accept that we cannot now put things right with the person who has died. Someone has died and now it is too late to make peace about that stupid argument or that missed visit; too late to apologize for that thoughtless remark; too late to just say that you really do love them. No matter how our common sense tells us that it is not our fault, guilt takes our hand and it appears that it will never let go. How can we cope with guilt – the 'if only' and 'I should have' and the 'why didn't I?'

Sometimes guilt may be compounded by the fact that there is an element of culpability in our feelings of guilt.

Perhaps we could have visited more, made more effort or cared more. Chapter 3 on Guilt and Grief will help you to find your way out of the 'guilt dilemma' and move on in your journey through grief.

Families in conflict

Conflicts in families are not erased when someone dies and old resentments can rise to the surface as emotions run high.

The sad fact is that the time of bereavement is an emotional time. It is a time when most of us suffer from mixed feelings – sorrow, yes, the most obvious emotion, but also perhaps relief, shame, guilt, distress, anger and bewilderment. When the family is thrown together all of these different emotions can fan into flames a fuse that was, perhaps, lit many years ago. The time of mourning can be a time of healing of old wounds but sometimes grief causes new disagreements to arise. Many family feuds can be traced back to a chance remark at a funeral or a disagreement over the contents of a will.

Personal effects

Chapter 6 on Personal Effects looks at the problem of what to do with all the personal possessions of the person who has died. These things are the tangible evidence of someone's existence. Disposing of personal effects after someone has died can be both complicated and emotionally devastating and sometimes the amount that needs to be disposed of and the emotions surrounding that task might feel overwhelming.

Some things are easier to dispose of than others and it isn't always the obvious things which we may find difficult to clear out. When is the best time to take on this task? If we are given a choice, should it be done immediately or can it wait a few months until we are able to think more clearly? We all have different ideas and thoughts of how to best deal with this problem. Some suggest that it might be better if you can resist the urge (and it is a common one) to dispose of things quickly. Not everything needs to be dealt with immediately and you may want to take your time over this, seeing it as a private task. Others will want the business of dealing with personal effects to be got 'out of the way' and are willing to allow others to sort things out and take decisions about what should be kept and what disposed of. This is one area where the internet can prove surprisingly helpful with the many selling and recycling sites giving an opportunity to pass on personal effects for the use of others. Often things turn up years after a death and remind us of our past grief in a surprising way.

Memorials

To many people, arranging a memorial is a vital part of the grieving process. There are many ways to remember the person you love and Chapter 7 on Memorials discusses some of the more unusual ones as well as the traditional. A memorial can vary from something simple like a memorial service which allows others who knew the person who has died to share their memories, to something complicated like setting up a charity in the name of the deceased. As technology moves along so do the different options that are available to us to raise memorials to those people whom we wish to remember. Disposing of ashes after cremation can amount to a memorial. Today we can have the ashes left after cremation fired into space, exploded in a firework or buried in a reef in the sea! Alternatively we can scatter someone's ashes in our garden under a rose bush, or have them made into diamond jewellery or glass ornaments. What do you want the memorial to achieve? Do you want some good to come out of the death or do you just need a place to go and spend time with the person who died? Is the memorial meant to be something that lasts down the generations or is it enough that those who are present now participate in the remembrance? Costs vary widely and we recommend waiting several months to make a decision where large sums of money are involved.

We all like to feel that when a crisis hits, our family are the ones we can rely on to support us – and what time could be more difficult than a time of bereavement? Often, though, those who are nearest to us seem only to add to our stress at this time.

The complications of today's extended families can be a cause of much heart-searching following a death. Should an ex-wife or husband be invited to a funeral, for example? Some might believe so and others not. Where should they sit during the service? With the family or in the main congregation?

Anniversaries

As the anniversaries loom, so does the sky seem to fill with dark clouds casting a shadow over us. Anniversaries are hard after bereavement and some can be very personal to us. As well as major events such as the first Christmas, the first birthday of the deceased, and anniversary of the death itself there are the small occasions in the life of every relationship which are just between those in the relationship. These occasions are more difficult to live through even than major anniversaries and it can take a long time until the pain of these moments fades.

Somehow we all find our way through this maze of the 'little anniversaries' in our own way. Some people may find a complete change of routine helps; others build new traditions to replace the old ones. The more public holidays such as Christmas (which is still a family occasion for many) may be especially difficult for many years after bereavement. What is the best way to spend an anniversary? We are able to give you some suggestions so that that day doesn't overshadow the year. Anniversaries are always with us, a recurring theme, but they do not have to dominate our thoughts and our actions in a way which makes us sad and depressed.

Beyond tomorrow

Our final chapter looks with you 'Beyond Tomorrow'. When in the throes of grief it may seem impossible to look beyond the immediate future. Often we can only get through this time by facing each day as it comes. Making any plans seems an impossible task. Indeed, we recommend that long-term plans are not made in a hurry or whilst undertaking the myriad of practical tasks which arise after a death. Sooner or later, though, the future has to be faced and Chapter 9 helps you to consider your options, to accept the new situation in which you find yourself and prepare your new script for life.

What lies beyond tomorrow for those who have recently been bereaved? A different stage with a different cast perhaps; new roles that will begin to feel more comfortable as time passes; and maybe...just maybe...some scenes that can bring you happiness again.

Chapter 1

Breaking Bad News

Breaking bad news is a task which is generally disliked and which many of us would avoid if at all possible. However, at some point during our lifetime many of us will find ourselves in the unenviable position of having to break bad news to family and friends. Telling others the news that someone whom they used to know has died must be the worst scenario we can imagine. This chapter is intended to support you through the process of breaking bad news.

The news that someone close to us has died has the potential to change lives. Every experience is different and individual and there is no 'one size fits all'. Bad news that is in some way expected (for example, because someone has been seriously ill for some time or is very elderly and in poor health) is still bad news. However, in these cases the element of shock will be less.

> Having to tell my husband the news and give him the same pain that I was feeling was the most heart-wrenching experience of my life.

People often imagine that they will be unlikely to be the bearer of bad news. The media tend to enforce this belief by relating scenes where police turn up on the doorstep to break the news that someone has been killed in an accident or by showing hospital scenes where doctors relay the news to stunned relatives. Of course these situations do occur. Many people die in hospital and in these cases a doctor or a nurse may have the unenviable task of breaking the news. It would be nice to think that these professional medical staff were trained in breaking bad news and that they carried out the task gently and compassionately. Unfortunately, the stories many people relate seem to indicate that this is not always the case.

> I walked into the ward and it seemed as if no one saw me. Nurses turned away and the other patients were all watching TV or seemingly asleep. Then the sister in charge came out from behind a screen. She stood there in the middle of the ward and shook her head at me. 'I'm afraid he didn't make it,' she said. That was how the news of my husband's death was broken to me.

The police and the armed forces personnel do have special training and in general break the news to relatives in a more acceptable manner.

Breaking the news of a death to those nearest to the deceased is only part of the story, however. For every death there are a number of people who need to be told the news so even if a professional person such as a police officer or a doctor has told the next of kin then there will be others in the family who need to be told, and this task can become the duty of anyone suddenly and without warning.

Most people feel a need to let others know the bad news as soon as possible. This seems to be an almost automatic reaction and indeed the act of continually stating the facts to a number of others may in a way be helpful because it may gradually make us believe it ourselves. The first reaction to news of a death is often disbelief.

I was reeling in shock after the death of my mother. Yet I realized that my brothers and sister had to be told the news and I didn't feel that I could ask anyone else to do that. I think now that I did the job very badly but it was as much as I could do to get the words out without bursting into tears.

My nephew phoned me to tell me that his father had died in hospital. My brother-in-law had seemed to be recovering from his accident but even so I am still appalled to think that my first words were, 'You're joking!' As if anyone would make such a joke. But it was an automatic response and luckily I don't think anyone really thought much about it.

There is another reason for letting people know the news as soon as conveniently possible. When in grief and shock we can all react badly and it is not unknown for relatives to feel slighted because they were told the news some time after death. One solution to the dilemma of letting as many people know as soon as possible is for two or three members of the family to undertake the task of breaking the news. This also has the advantage of spreading the stress load for each person. You could also ask each person that you tell to pass the news on to one or two named other people so that the message is disseminated more quickly and less stressfully.

Bad news that comes completely out of the blue needs very careful handling, and when we ourselves have been the recipient and now have to pass it on to others it is a traumatic and unwelcome task.

> I was completely taken aback at my father's funeral to be confronted by my aunts, his two sisters, who were furious because I had telephoned their brother before them. Why this made a difference I don't know. We informed everyone on the same day but it seems they had been comparing notes and worked out that my uncle was telephoned on the morning of the death whilst they were informed in the afternoon. They felt that they had been somehow relegated in importance but I had been simply working through my address book.

Bad news will not go away and we may not be able to delegate the task of breaking bad news to others, nor may we feel that we should.

> I wondered for one brief foolish moment whether there was any way that I could prevent him from hearing this terrible news.

There are many ways of communicating these days and we hear of incidents where people are given unwelcome news such as the news of redundancy by email or by text. Breaking bad news is so difficult that we may be sorely tempted to take the easy way out and convey it in an impersonal way like this, thus saving ourselves the distress of dealing with another person's shock, bewilderment and questions. However, this is absolutely not acceptable. Needless to say, the news of a death should always be given to someone personally, preferably face-to-face, although of course you may need to give the news by telephone. In some circumstances you may need to send the news in writing and in these circumstances you should attend to this as soon as possible.

> My husband was sent an email telling him that his best friend had died of a heart attack the day before. Fortunately I read the email before my husband did so I was able to give him the bad news and he was devastated. I can't understand why we weren't given this news by phone – the four of us had been close friends and we'd had dinner together only the week before.

Email can be useful as a means to prepare people and to ask them to get in touch. 'Can you call me please, I need to speak to you urgently?' for example. Details about the funeral can also be given by email to save time but *only* after the news itself has been given by word of mouth. Funeral arrangements can also legitimately be conveyed by a short printed note or a newspaper announcement if there are likely to be many people who would like to attend.

Newspaper announcements (obituary notices) are useful to let the wider community know about a death and they also allow the bereaved to give some outlet to their feelings by such words as 'sadly missed' or 'much mourned by his wife and family'. These days it is permissible to use social media (Facebook, etc.) in this way as well but this method should be saved strictly for the wider community and every effort should be made to first tell any family and friends by telephone or in person.

Breaking bad news over the phone

How you break news of a death over the telephone must of course depend upon to whom you are speaking and whether they have any inkling of the news you are about to convey. It might be important to find out if the person you are speaking to is alone or if there is someone with them. If you are calling on a mobile telephone it is also worth making sure that the recipient is not driving or in a public place. If they are, ask them to call you back as soon as they can safely do so *before* you break the news. Before you pick up the phone take a few seconds to compose yourself, whether you are a professional or someone who has yourself received devastating news. The person you will be phoning will remember this call for ever. If you are on the phone your facial expression will be reflected in your voice, as the Samaritans will tell you.

On the telephone you might say: 'Hello Mary, this is Jane. Is there someone with you? I need to speak to you for just a moment. It's very important. I wish I could tell you this in person but I am afraid I have some bad news.'

It might make it easier if you acknowledge the last contact they had with the person who has died, before stating that you are about to deliver bad news: 'I know we had dinner with Jennifer last week but I'm afraid I have some bad news.'

If the news is not unexpected you might say:

'You know of course that Mum was very ill last night...'

'I know the doctor had told you he might not last more than a day or two...'

'When you last saw John he was very weak and I'm afraid that this morning we heard...'

When we are feeling anxious we have a tendency to speak rapidly, perhaps in order to get the ordeal over with, so be aware of this tendency and try to slow down your speech.

If the person on other end of the telephone is very distressed an empathic response might be:

'I know that it is very upsetting for you to hear this news, particularly by telephone.'

A response to a person who repeatedly says 'It's not true, it's impossible!' could be 'I know this must be a terrible shock for you'.

If someone goes very quiet or simply says 'Thank you for letting me know' you might reply:

'I know this news has stunned/shocked you. Would you like me to stay on the line for a while?'

Denial is a way of coping, so if someone seemingly does not understand consider that they may simply not be able to absorb the news. Sometimes it can help to repeat the news in a different way or to give some further details to allow the hearer to collect themselves and be able to respond:

'As I said, Jennifer was taken ill very suddenly. We are all so shocked, especially as we had dinner with her last week and she seemed so well.'

'It was really very sudden.'

'The doctor says that no one could have predicted she would collapse so quickly.'

If the person you are speaking to is tearful, and particularly if they are alone, offer to call anyone they may want to be with them. Suggest you call back or they call you after an agreed period of time when they have had some time to digest the news. You could offer to pass it on to people they may want to tell or ask to come and stay with them.

If strong emotions are not acknowledged you may appear insensitive. An empathic response is important in order to acknowledge the pain the other person is feeling.

Silence

Many people find silence on the telephone very uncomfortable, especially after breaking bad news. Silence also feels much longer on the phone and using comforting sounds and words, like 'Take your time – I'm still here' can help you to break the silence until the person feels able to speak.

Be prepared to repeat what has happened as often as required. Some people need to hear it over and over again.

> My husband died very young and very suddenly and I found myself emotionally unable to pass this news to our family and friends. I asked a close family friend who happened to be a doctor to do this on my behalf.

When you give wider acquaintances the news of a death often the first question they will ask is for details of the funeral arrangements. Therefore, except for family and very close friends, it can be worth waiting a day or two to break the news so that you can give these details and save another round of phone calls.

Breaking bad news face-to-face

If you are telling someone bad news face-to-face, try to compose your own expression. Make sure you are in a private environment and not a room that people will be using to come and go or where you will be interrupted:

- If there is a television on, ask if you can turn it off.
- Adopt an open posture (not folded arms nor hands on hips headteacher style).
- Make sure your mobile phone or beeper is turned off and you have no interruptions.
- It is best if you are both seated before the news is broken. If possible it is better if there is nothing between you and the person you are speaking to, not even a table.
- Lean forward.
- Make eye contact, however difficult this may be.

- It is good to prepare slightly – for example, 'I'm afraid I have very bad news'. But after this you should break the news without unnecessary preamble.

Medical professionals

If you are a medical professional you may have had to break bad news often, and although it is likely that you are distressed and feel for those to whom you are breaking the news you may feel that it is important not to show emotion and to keep a professional manner. Nothing could be further than the truth. If you do not show emotion sometimes the overall impression given is that you do not care. It will seem to them that the death of someone they care for is not important to you or to those who have been caring for and tending to them.

There is a lot of evidence about non-verbal language being more important in certain circumstances than the words used, and if your tone and facial expression are cold you will seem uncaring.

> I believe the doctor was really embarrassed at having to tell me – or maybe he was just inexperienced. He skirted round the subject for several minutes and eventually used such technical language – medical terms which I couldn't take in – that it was a good few minutes after he had left me that I really understood what had happened. I had to ask the nurse whether he really meant that my father was dead.

Historically it was believed that the way to break bad news was to launch into the whole story before ending with the death. However, this is unnecessarily cruel. So, do not say: 'Fred was found unconscious last night and an ambulance was called by a neighbour and he was taken to hospital…'

This approach encourages the hearer to believe that he is still alive (where there's life there is hope) and as long as you delay telling them he is not, the more time they have to build up hope.

Instead, say: 'I'm afraid I have bad news about Fred (warning shot). He died last night (fact). He was found unconscious in his bedroom and died in hospital (repeating fact with a bit more information).' Further details can follow when they are asked for.

Whatever your own feelings (you may be tired, impatient, annoyed or under pressure) take the time to add something that shows that you and your colleagues care:

'I'm really very sorry.'

'We did all we could but he didn't regain consciousness.'

'We are very sad to lose him.'

'Please ask me any questions you like.'

Breaking bad news in residential homes

In spite of the fact that end of life is very much a part of life, particularly in residential and nursing homes for the elderly, the 'empty chair syndrome' still seems to rule in many homes. Edna who often sits with Joan sees Joan's chair empty at breakfast but thinks perhaps she is sleeping late. At lunchtime when her chair is still empty she asks a care worker 'Where is Joan? Is she not feeling well?' only to be told that Joan died during the night. How does Edna feel? Is she not significant enough to be told that her friend has died? Does no one recognize that she will have feelings of sadness and grief? Treatment like this may lead her to wonder what will happen when she dies. Will no one speak of her passing?

One reason why often residents are not told of their friend's passing is that there is an outdated belief that it will make them think about their own end of life. However, it is important to realize that most of the residents not only think about the end of their lives but are often well prepared for death. Generally speaking, the older people become the more prepared for death they are. Perhaps their relatives are not ready for them to die but often they themselves are mentally and emotionally packed and ready for their journey.

There are some homes where a close companion will be told of her friend's passing, but it seems to be fairly hit and miss. As we mentioned in our book *End of Life: The Essential Guide to Caring* (2010) there needs to be a change in policy. There should be good systems in place so that staff are informed of the news in a timely manner as they come on duty and before they have contact with residents.

Every home should have an 'End of Life Lead' and he/she should take responsibility for breaking the news, remembering that care workers are likely to become attached to those whom they care for. Off-duty staff should be telephoned so that no one is left uninformed. Care staff are likely to experience many more deaths than the average person and the emotional stress this entails should be borne in mind. Suitable support should be offered to staff if required.

Residents should also be told individually and supported if necessary. Those suffering from dementia may not remember the news but they still have a right to be told.

Care homes should also consider how they might remember those who have died. There is a very important point here. A resident who sees a deceased companion quickly forgotten will know that when their turn comes they too will be hastily taken out of the back door and their memory erased. We know that the way others are treated will be the way we will be treated too. There is much talk about treating older people with dignity and respect during their life but we should also treat the dead with dignity and respect. It is so easy for older people to lose their sense of self-worth. One of the key principles in good mental health is a sense of 'agency' – a sense of having a place in the world, a feeling that we have a part to play, a feeling that we contribute to society.

I go into care and nursing homes a lot in the course of my job. Very few of them have any sort of quiet room, memorial board or book or anything which seems to acknowledge people after their death. I think it is a shame. Everyone who goes into a care home would surely like to think that they will be remembered by the staff as well as by their own relatives. No one likes to imagine that they are just 'passing through' to be cared for and forgotten about.

At the home where my mother spent her last days they have a 'memory day' in January when they put up photos of those who have died in the past year. The local vicar holds a prayer service for anyone who wants to attend. A surprising number do. Afterwards they have a tea party where people exchange memories. You would think it would be a sad occasion but the residents enjoy it.

The Christmas card effect

It is worth remembering here the 'Christmas card effect'. In many cases after a death the first Christmas brings cards and greetings from people who have not yet received the news. Many of us have 'Christmas card' acquaintances – in other words friends or ex-colleagues with whom we only have occasional contact. The first contact from these may not of course come at Christmas, but this is a common time. Sometimes it is only when the first Christmas comes around that we may realize the full extent of the deceased's social network. It may seem really awkward to notify the sender of a Christmas card or the person who sends an unexpected letter or email months after the death that the person they are contacting is now deceased.

If a card arrives at Christmas it is probably more sensitive to wait until after the festive season to make contact, but in any case it is kind to let people know the news even if it is several months old. You can say something simple like: 'I'm sorry to have to tell you that Joan died in the summer. Unfortunately, I did not have your contact details or I would have let you know before this.' If you know something about the past you could add some mention of this: 'She always remembered you from her schooldays and often spoke of you.'

It is worth doing this small chore, however upsetting, or cards or messages may continue to arrive and to cause distress.

Other people to notify

This might be the place to mention the many people and organizations who need to be notified of a death. These are not direct acquaintances or in the immediate social circle and notification can sometimes wait until after the funeral, but nevertheless it needs to be done. The list includes utility companies, banks, libraries, the vehicle licensing authority, the passport office, the tax authority, social clubs, support organizations (such as the Stroke Association, cancer support groups or the Alzheimer's Society perhaps), the local church if attended and car breakdown organizations. You will also need to cancel any upcoming hospital or dental appointments (health departments do not always talk to each other effectively).

Cancelling appointments and informing businesses and professionals can be harrowing so this may be a time to ask relatives or friends to assist you.

Chapter 2

Breaking Bad News to Children, People with Intellectual Disabilities and People with Dementia

Breaking bad news to children

> When the doctor came out of my mother's bedroom I was waiting at the bottom of the stairs. 'Your mother is dying,' he said, 'you do realize that.'
>
> It was the first time anyone had mentioned that fact to me but I answered, 'Yes I do.'
>
> The news was totally devastating, and from that moment my whole world fell apart. I no longer had the luxury of being a child. She died three days later. I'd had no preparation at all.

Historically we were told children should be seen and not heard. They were not considered to be important, relevant or aware enough to be told of an impending death or invited to participate in the funeral.

Many 'children' now in their 70s and 80s bitterly resented being excluded from the funeral of a parent or beloved grandparent or having been 'sent away' when a parent was dying and upon their return no mention being made of the parent who died. Not surprisingly this has thrown a shadow that has influenced their entire lives.

Over the years, there has been increasing interest in understanding what constitutes a child's emotional and physical wellbeing along with the realization that what happens in childhood becomes part of the adult.

We in the western world live with a paradox: death is all around us, yet we believe that if we do not talk with children about death, it will not touch them. We try to protect and insulate them from this fact of life, which is typically associated with anxiety and pain (Silverman 1999).

My mother died quite suddenly when I was seven. My father told me she had died and that I was to go before the funeral and stay with my grandparents on my father's side. I hardly knew them as they lived in Scotland. I stayed with them for a month. They were very nice to me but didn't mention my mother once. Upon my return home I was told to be brave and I went back to school. I don't know if the school were informed but no one mentioned it to me. Thirty years later when my daughter was seven, I had a breakdown and with professional support I was finally able to grieve for my mother.

Keeping children out of the loop is often counterproductive. All too often children do know that there is something wrong. Being excluded from the facts can lead them to believe or imagine that in some way they may be responsible for whatever this bad thing is that is happening. In addition, their peers are unlikely to have had this experience so they cannot get support from them. So if the adults in their life are not talking to them the child feels entirely isolated and is left with no one to turn to. The more the child is allowed to be involved, the more likely they are to have a healthy grieving process and the less likely they are to have delayed trauma.

It is thought that children under five years of age (approximately) do not really understand the concept of death in that they are unable to realize the finality of death. They may need help in understanding that the person who has died will not be coming back. It is important not to use jargon here or phrases such as 'gone to heaven' or 'gone to sleep'. The words 'died' and 'death' are important. Their limited understanding may lead to a lack of reaction when told about a death and the implication of the news may take several months to be realized.

Older children can begin to understand the concept but may need careful explanations and support. You may need to repeat the facts over and over again. This helps children to begin to process the information and builds trust in the adults around them. They may have an increased awareness of their own mortality, and fear for their own safety; and they may fear the death of the other parent and will need reassurance. However, don't be surprised if the child appears not to react to bad news or immediately starts talking or playing with something. They will find their own way to absorb the news and tend to alternate between showing awareness of the situation and appearing to be distracted by something else. Ask the child what they want to know about what happened. Their questions will show you what they have understood from your words. If they do not ask anything, encourage them to repeat what they have heard. Be honest about what you do not know.

Adolescents understand the concept of death; however, their reaction may be complicated by the struggles of adolescence. This is the time when adolescents separate from their parents and having a parent die can be very difficult. An added complication can be that relationships between adolescents and parents are often strained and their last memory of any conversation with the dead parent may have been of a time of conflict. Adolescents may talk at length about death, but seldom to those closest to them in the family. They will often use their peers as support.

However, all children deserve to be informed about death. If children are given age-appropriate information, although distressing, it will help them to feel empowered and a part of the drama instead of an unwitting and unwilling member of the audience.

> I was about four or five when my paternal grandmother died. I now know that she had been ill for some time but I cannot remember whether I realized it then. What I remember most is that my younger sister (probably aged about three) and I saw our two older sisters crying and asked them why they were doing so. They said, 'Nanny has died.' But neither my younger sister nor I really understood why they were crying.

It is natural for parents to be so overwhelmed by an impending death that they themselves are unable to think straight. There are no lessons in our schools that prepare us for the type of news that changes our entire future landscape, so it is not altogether surprising that parents do not recognize the needs of their children, or perhaps feel that they wish to give them a normal life and to protect them for as long as possible. It is also natural for parents to feel that they cannot cope with their own emotions, let alone the emotions of their children.

Much as we may want to, we cannot protect children from harsh realities of life and sometimes it may be worth asking oneself the question: 'Who are we protecting?' Are you perhaps protecting yourself from having to deal with the hurt, the fear, the questions and emotions of your children? You cannot protect children from the fact that people and pets get ill and then die. The only question is how well will you, and they, deal with it. Treating death as a natural extension of life is an early lesson well learned, albeit a very painful one.

Trust is a crucial component in any relationship, especially one between children and their parents. Breaking trust over a situation as critical as this one will have long-lasting consequences for the parent who remains alive.

> I was an only child and very introverted. My dog was my best friend. We were constant companions and inseparable. One day when I got home from school my mother told me that she had given my dog to someone who lived in the country. I was utterly devastated. About 20 years later she told me the truth – that the dog had cancer and she had had him put down. If she had given me the bad news at the time and made me a party to the illness and subsequent death I would have been absolutely distraught but our relationship would have survived. She said she had tried to protect me. But what had she protected me from?

So how much should you tell children and at what point should you have this conversation?

It is best to get advice from professionals involved whenever possible.

When it comes to breaking the news, overloading a child with information may be doing exactly that – overloading them. If death is possible but the prognosis is not known and the parent is undergoing treatment, it may be advisable to break the news into chunks. First: 'Mummy isn't well. She is having some treatment and won't be feeling well for a while.' If the prognosis then changes because the treatment isn't working, another chunk of information can be given to the child: 'Mummy isn't well and the treatment isn't helping her as well as we hoped.'

And finally if necessary the child can be told of their mother's end-of-life prognosis. It will be devastating and probably the worst conversation you will ever have but for the child it will avoid the sudden shock which adds an additional devastating blow and an additional complication to grief. It will at least allow them to feel a part of what is going on.

Any conversation should be in an appropriate environment. Having this conversation in a hospital waiting room or sterile environment doesn't help. You should of course make sure there are no interruptions or interference from televisions or mobile phones.

Find out what the child already knows. For example, you could start by asking, 'What do you know about your mum's illness?'

You can use sentences like:

'The doctor is worried because mummy isn't getting any better.'

'The doctor told mummy that the treatment isn't working any more.'

'Would you like to know more?' (Thus allowing the child to have some control over how much they hear.) It is important to respect the child's wish to know more. However, if death is imminent you may not have that luxury.

'That means that mummy will die soon.'

When breaking such news to children it is very important to not use euphemisms such as 'We've lost your dad' or

'Mummy's gone to sleep'. Children may not understand these and may take them literally.

The right of children to go to funerals has been much debated over the years but again there is a belief that by preventing them from going to funerals we are protecting them from death being a part of life. Funerals are a crucial end-of-life ceremony and they are important for a healthy grieving process. Therefore children should be given a choice whenever age-appropriate. Having conversations about children going to funerals should take place prior to the death whenever possible.

In cases of suicide or violent death it is strongly advised that the family receive professional therapeutic help. If it is possible to have a professional present when the news is broken this may be helpful.

After a death, it is important to inform the relevant teachers and staff at the child's school and ask for their support for the child.

Crying in front of children is natural, but it is important to explain why you are crying so that the child doesn't think it is because of something that they have done. The same applies if you are feeling depressed or sad. It is much better to explain, 'Mummy is crying/upset because she is sad that Daddy died/is dying' than to try to pretend that nothing has happened.

Telling a child to be brave, or admiring their braveness, can cause them to hide their grief as they want to appear to be brave and this is counterproductive. Grief is a natural reaction and it is natural for both child and parent to grieve.

The way in which children react and understand will be influenced by their age, their life experience, their emotional maturity and their family's cultural and spiritual beliefs. Boys and girls often grieve in different ways.

After death you should explain what will happen next, including where the body will be. You can say that they can visit again later and perhaps might like to bring some mementos to leave with the body, though you need to be careful that it doesn't sound as if the dead person will be aware of what has been brought.

Children can ask difficult questions and you may not be able to satisfy all of them. Be honest and say something like: 'We don't know any more at the moment, but as soon as we do know we will tell you.' This will stop the child from feeling something is being deliberately kept from them.

It is precisely because children don't understand all the implications that we need to talk to and include them. Above all, make sure it is clear that the death can in no way be attributed to the child's behaviour. Such thoughts as 'I shouted at my mum and now she's dead' can colour a child's mind for ever.

Breaking bad news to people with an intellectual disability

There is no one way to break bad news to people with an intellectual disability just as there is no one way to break bad news to anyone else. Nor is breaking bad news a one-time event for those with an intellectual disability – it is a process which involves repetition, and it is this that enables a slow build-up of understanding.

> Death is not frightening, it is normal and we try and make it normal so we don't make a drama of it. A lot of the residents rely on routine. And so even if someone dies you can't change the routine because that will upset everyone in the house.

Between us (Liz Hayes and Becky Morris, managers of a small home in Surrey) we have been managing this home for about 11 years. There are 12 residents in the home. We have had three different deaths here. Jonathan's death was expected after a deterioration of over a year with dementia (see *End of Life: The Essential Guide to Caring*, Chapter 6). Robert's* death was very, very sudden and Jane* died after a short illness. So in a sense the home has experienced three very different types of death. With the two expected deaths we sat with the residents in the dining room very informally. We explained that the person was very unwell and asked if they understood what that means, and then we told them that that person won't be with us for very much longer and asked is there anything they wanted to us to do to support them. We decided that that was the way to break bad news to them – support and include them in every step. I don't think they necessarily understand what death means or the finality of it and I don't think there is a way of explaining what death is. (*These names have been changed.)

There are some rules that apply to other people that do not apply to people with an intellectual disability. For example, in Chapter 1 we stated that it would be wise to fire a warning shot before telling someone of a significant sudden death. This does not apply to people with an intellectual disability.

For people with an intellectual disability, news that their routine is unavoidably changed or cancelled can be more upsetting than news that someone has died. Routine is critical, and people with an intellectual disability need a great deal of support in coping with life's changes.

Many people with an intellectual disability find it very difficult to understand new information and to learn new skills. They also may not have a concept of time and therefore telling them that a resident is ill and will die may be taken as meaning that they are going to die immediately. They may not understand the concept of death or they may want to know exactly when that person is going to die.

The same would apply if they were told that they themselves were not going to live much longer – they might want to know exactly when they were going to die.

The language that is used for breaking bad news must be very clear. Euphemisms such as 'passed on' or 'passed away' can be misinterpreted. The words 'dead' or 'died' should be used so that there is no opportunity for misunderstanding.

I think people in care manage it better because most of them don't see their family any more, and although the core staff here has been with us for years there are care staff who leave and others replace them so they have had a continuous experience of loss. I think also residents are used to people disappearing – they don't grieve because they know someone is going to come along and take that space. Whereas we can't replace a family or friend for them, it seems that everyone in their life is replaceable and as long as their life and routine doesn't change they seem to be able to cope with death.

Our first death, Robert, died on the spot – there was no warning at all. We (the two managers) went to the hospital and then we went to Bognor to tell his parents at 2.00 in the morning. When we returned to the home we met with the staff and the residents in the dining room, we allowed them to go into Robert's room and said that if anyone wanted to go and see him in the hospital to say goodbye then we would make sure they were able to do that. The residents didn't want to, but the staff went because his death was such a shock and we needed to see him and say goodbye.

Even though some of the residents had lived with the three who died for many years we saw no sign of them grieving. They often reminisce about the people who died but they didn't grieve and their life carried on as normal.

The only time in all our years of managing this home that I have ever seen a resident cry was when her rabbits were eaten by a fox. She was inconsolable and wanted them buried properly and she was very sad and subdued. Her rabbits affected her more than the three people who died, even though one of the residents had been very close to her. They seem to know what people expect of them around death but emotionally they don't seem to grieve. I think also we try and protect them as much as possible. We know how hard it is for us when someone dies and their lives are difficult enough having to live in care without contact from their family, so we don't want them to feel bad. Because a lot of people don't know what happens after death we have asked each member of staff to spend a day with the undertakers so that if necessary they can explain to the residents what happens next.

In her book, *How to Break Bad News to People with Intellectual Disabilities*, Irene Tuffrey-Wijne states that we need to help people live with a changed and changing reality rather than breaking bad news in one instant. Helping them build knowledge by breaking complex information down into singular chunks of information. She states that building a foundation is key. In this way, step-by-step and over a period of time, the person with learning disabilities builds their understanding of the way their situation is changing because of the bad news.

The people around them support this by giving small, singular chunks of information that make sense to the person. This does not have to be done by talking: much of the information will be understood through experience.

Some of these chunks will be 'background knowledge' – for example, 'Nurses make ill people better', 'Cancer can kill you'. Some will be about what is happening right now – for example, 'Dad is not eating much', 'Dad's bed is downstairs'. And some is information that will take place in the future, which is more difficult to understand – for example, 'Dad will be too ill to talk to me' and 'Dad may have to go into hospital'. You don't have to tell them everything (remember chunks) but don't lie.

Irene Tuffrey-Wijne gives ten guiding questions:

- Does the person have capacity?

- What knowledge does he possess already?

- What size are the knowledge chunks he can cope with?

- How many more chunks of knowledge can he be helped to understand?

- Is he able to understand this specific chunk of information at this point in time?

- Is it important that he understands this specific information NOW?

- What is the best way/place/time to give the person the best chance of understanding?

- Who can best help him to understand?

- What and who does he need in order to communicate in the best way?

- Can he be harmed by receiving this chunk of knowledge at this point of time?

(2012, pp.170–172)

> When we plan the funeral we encourage the residents to have a say in how they want it to be and of course we allow anyone who wants to go to a funeral and we try to include them in everything.

There is no reason for people with an intellectual disability to be excluded from a funeral. Again, it is very much a person-centred decision that should be made by those who know them best and it is important that they attend with someone who knows them well so they are fully supported.

Breaking bad news to people with dementia

Should you tell a person with dementia that someone close to them has died? The general rule of thumb is that if the person died many years ago it is preferable not to, because they knew the news, and their memory impairment has caused them to forget. Reminding them will be as though they are hearing it again for the first time. However, if the person recently died the following is relevant.

One of the first rules when caring for someone with dementia is not to add to their levels of stress. You might think that telling them bad news will be stressful for them. You might also think that there is little point in telling them. Won't they just forget? Will they really understand?

The question of whether to break the news about a death usually arises when someone with dementia is living in a residential care home. Those people with dementia still living at home will be aware of the bad news because they will overhear phone calls, be party to the lead-up to death (visits to hospital, ambulance calling, etc.) or possibly even be there at the scene of death. In such cases never make the mistake of thinking that the person with dementia has not understood what has happened and can therefore be ignored or not involved in discussions about funeral arrangements and so on. Remember that in the slow deterioration within the brain the emotions remain until the end. The person with dementia may forget *why* they are sad but they will be aware that they *feel* sad and this will make them anxious. They may want to be with you constantly or they may start to pace around or be generally less settled than usual at the very time you may be hoping for some quiet reflection yourself.

The best thing to do in this situation is reassure the person with dementia and remind them occasionally of what has happened: 'Yes, you feel sad because Joe has died. We all miss him.'

Try to keep the routine as much as usual and speak calmly and quietly. Do not ask difficult questions but involve them in the arrangements. For example, do not say (unless you feel they are able to still make decisions), 'Do you think Vera would have liked "All things bright and beautiful" as one of the hymns at her funeral?' But instead say, 'We are going to sing "All things bright and beautiful" at Vera's funeral. It was a hymn she always liked.' It is also worth remembering that times of stress and difficulty may bring latent thoughts to the surface which should not be ignored. For example, the person with dementia may wonder who will look after them now if their main carer has died. They may ask you what seems like a trivial question 'Who will drive Margaret to our house now?' because, in this example, to them the main focus of their mind is that the person who has died used to bring their daughter to visit.

You could answer, 'Margaret is going to drive herself here. She will be coming tomorrow.' In this way you will be trying to answer the unspoken anxiety 'Will Margaret be coming to see me any more?' instead of the actual apparently unimportant question.

There is no reason to hide your own sadness if you are sad, although it may upset the person with dementia if they see you cry. In this case it may be best to just explain simply, 'I'm feeling a bit sad about Joe dying.' And leave it at that.

Try not to be upset if the person with dementia actually says something socially unacceptable: 'It's a good thing he died – I never liked him, you know.' Although many people with dementia keep their social abilities for a long time and understand what is acceptable comment, others do not. People with frontal lobe dementia especially may be quite outspoken and say exactly what is on their mind. It is reasonable to say 'Please don't say that. It upsets me' although this may not be effective, but it is probably a waste of time to show too much shock or try to reason on the grounds of 'We don't speak ill of the dead'. You could say 'You will upset Margaret very much if you say that to her' and this may work but, just in case, you may like to warn visitors ahead of their visit about possible upsetting comments which may be made.

It is very possible that the person with dementia may forget what has happened or may not be able to understand the finality of death. One man constantly said to the care workers in the home where he lived, 'Yes, I understand that my wife is dead. You have told me before. But is she coming to see me today?' Others may ask 'Is Joe coming today?' with monotonous regularity so that you want to scream at them to make them understand. The best thing to do is develop a 'stuck record' approach but add some reassurance: 'No, Joe has died, remember. He won't be coming to see us because he has died. But Margaret will be coming next week.'

A few weeks after our daughter died, I went to tell my ex-husband who was in a home some distance from where I lived. I took with me a picture of our daughter and told him, 'Our daughter is dead.' He looked at the picture and smiled and said, 'Oh, but she has been here with me for a long time.'

You have to keep in mind that the person with dementia cannot control what they remember and what they forget. If they laugh at a joke, enjoy a television programme or say they are looking forward to an outing they are not being insensitive. They are responding to what they remember at the time. It is best to just accept this behaviour and certainly not to see it as disrespectful or a sign that they do not care about what has happened.

I remember that when my father-in-law died his daughter, Molly, came to stay with her mother for a few days. My mother-in-law had dementia. Molly confided in me one day that she thought her mother had never loved her father because she was still laughing at the comedy on television and didn't seem to want to discuss the funeral. I was a bit surprised that Molly didn't understand her mother's condition.

It is definitely not a good idea to try to hide what has happened or to make arrangements in secret. The person with dementia will be aware of something going on and be more anxious, and more upset, if they think that you are keeping secrets from them. It is a very bad mistake to do this as you will be adding to the fears and anxieties which are never far away from someone with dementia. In addition you will probably not be able to keep up the pretence or someone else may 'let the cat out of the bag' with upsetting results.

> My brother knew that Dan had dementia. Usually he was kind and gentle with him and often took him out to the pub or for fishing trips. However, at my sister Mary's funeral things became very awkward. Dan kept asking when we were going to go home and began to be very loud and aggressive. My brother was already quite upset and he suddenly turned on Dan and shouted, 'Why don't you show some respect, you rotter? Don't you care at all?' The worst of it was that, unable to understand what he had done wrong, Dan burst out laughing. I don't know whether he thought it was a joke or just didn't know how to react. I had to take him home in a hurry. Afterwards my brother was mortified but I don't think Dan remembered the incident at all.

There are many occasions when it is actually unkind to remind someone that their close relative is dead. Sometimes the person with dementia seems to be living in their own 'shadow-world' of the past. They may believe that they are still young and be convinced that their mother and father are still alive. If a wife or husband has died, the person with dementia may never really remember this and continue to cook meals for them, or tell you they are 'down in the shed in the garden' or in some other such place. If you respond by saying 'No, Mum, he is dead' it may cause real upset. It is as if the person with dementia is hearing it for the first time every time you say it. Imagine how you would feel if someone suddenly said that someone close to you has died when you had forgotten this and simply assumed that they were in another room somewhere. In circumstances like this it is best just to let the remark pass. After a few moments it is very likely that the person with dementia will recall the fact for themselves or they might be distracted by something else.

> After my uncle died, my aunt seemed often to be unaware of this fact. She would explain away his absence by saying he had gone to the shops or was digging his allotment. One day she told me about a terrible dream she had had the night before in which a funeral car pulled up at the door and she was driven to a funeral service and my uncle was cremated. At the end of this account she suddenly shivered and said, 'Thank goodness it was only a dream.' I didn't know how to respond.

If the person with dementia is living in a residential home when someone close to them dies, it may be tempting to keep them in ignorance of the fact 'because it might upset them unnecessarily'. It is understandable that this notion may be considered. If the person with dementia is settled in the home and seems happy it might seem cruel to disturb that equilibrium, especially if the news can be kept from them successfully. This is the important point. If the person who has died was a regular visitor it may be impossible to keep the death a secret. Even if the person with dementia appears not to recognize visitors, or is unable to name them, they probably know they are familiar people. They may well experience pleasure at the visit and feel better afterwards. Even if they are unable to actually ask why the visitor no longer comes, they may sense that something is wrong. The loss of the ability to put feelings into words does not necessarily indicate the loss of feeling.

One elderly man in the care home where I worked was frequently visited by his daughter and her children – his grandchildren. When his grand-daughter died in a car accident he was informed. His daughter continued to visit with her other child and it seemed as if this man didn't register any change. But one day, a couple of months after the death, another resident had a visit from a small girl relative and this man became very upset, shouting incoherently and crying and upsetting the little girl. We thought afterwards that he was just expressing his feelings about the death of his grandchild – there was no other way he could tell us how he was feeling.

It is probably best in such cases to tell the truth. Of course there will be upset feelings and sadness, but sadness is normal and appropriate after a death. In such cases be sure to take the staff of the home into your confidence and warn them when you are going to break the news. They can then be prepared for any unusual behaviour or even take the time to help the person with dementia express their grief in the best way for them. You can tell the staff that you will be happy for them to talk about the loss if the person with dementia appears to want that.

If someone is very severely affected with dementia and no longer responds to visitors or seems to recognize them, it may be better to conceal the truth. However, it is important if any concealment takes place to make sure that there is no possibility of any chance remarks giving this secret away. It is also a good idea to tell the care home staff what you are planning and make sure that they too understand what should not be spoken of. It is easy for inexperienced staff to believe that an unresponsive person doesn't take in what they are gossiping about whilst making the bed!

One lady with dementia living in a care home began asking the new manager where her husband was. The new manager had been told that the husband had died many years before but wasn't sure whether she should mention this or not. She prevaricated, promising to check the records and find out where he was, hoping the resident would forget her question. But the questions continued. Eventually she had to say, 'I'm very sorry, Linda, but your husband died several years ago.' The lady replied, 'Yes, they told me that, but I thought I'd check to see if you knew.'

Chapter 3

Guilt and Grief

My mother died in most unpleasant circumstances in hospital and for days afterwards I couldn't lie down to sleep without going over and over in my head the hours and days leading up to the moment of death and trying to work out what I could have done to change what happened. I still sometimes have these feelings. They come unbidden into my head without warning and I am no nearer to coming to terms with the guilt I feel, although logically I know nothing I did could have made a difference.

Guilt

Grief and guilt seem to go hand-in-hand. In the first few days after death the survivors are often left with an immediate sense of guilt. Thoughts seem to run through our minds unbidden:

'If only I had said I thought something was wrong.'

'I should have spent more time with her.'

'I didn't tell him I loved him when I left on that last day.'

Our minds are full of the 'If only' and the 'It was my fault' and 'I could have done more'.

Often these thoughts have an element of truth. Perhaps we could have visited our mother more often. Maybe our last hospital visit *was* rushed because we had another appointment. Possibly if we had drawn attention to a shortcoming on the part of hospital staff things might have gone differently. The point is, we cannot know if that change in our behaviour might have made a difference. How often do we read reports in the newspaper of some suggested neglect on the part of hospital staff only to read the coroner's final verdict that 'despite these shortcomings (or this neglect, or these mistakes) there would have been no difference in the outcome. X would still have died'.

A coroner can make a statement like this. That is their job. It is more difficult for a relative left behind after the death, grieving and feeling guilty. Sometimes it is impossible to acknowledge our feelings of guilt. Suppose your listener agreed with you that you should feel guilty? Would that be more devastating or would it be a relief?

Following any death there is an enormous gap in the lives of those left behind and there may seem to be an even bigger gap when someone dies after a long illness or dementia. This feeling of emptiness can cause additional complicated feelings of guilt. One may feel guilt about the impatience felt whilst the person was alive, guilt about the events leading to death, guilt about the relief from the carer's burden, guilt about the place of death if it was in a hospital or a nursing home. Almost everyone feels guilt after a death, and a protracted illness does not give any exemption to these feelings but rather may intensify them.

Guilt may take different forms. Many of us carry a feeling of guilt throughout our life. Guilt is a necessary emotion in many ways. How can a child be brought up to understand that others have feelings and that they can be hurt by his or her actions unless the emotion of guilt is used? Without a natural notion of guilt we would walk roughshod over other people's feelings and perhaps even physically hurt them. Psychopathic people do not feel guilt for their actions and this makes it possible for them to carry out what seem unspeakable acts.

However, a deep-seated feeling of guilt can colour someone's whole life and make them unable ever to enjoy innocent pleasures. Where this is the case it is possible for someone to be consumed with guilt even where there is no logical reason for this emotion. In a case like this a person may feel guilty in an unspecified way after the death of someone they love. They may say that they feel guilty, but on closer questioning they are unable to state clearly their reasons for this guilt. These feelings of guilt are not as simple as the feelings which affect us and cause us to question whether anything we could have done would have avoided the death or made the passing easier for the one who has died.

Many people find it difficult to express their love for someone. In particular some have an ambivalent relationship with their parents. Love and respect for our parents seems to be assumed by society. It is assumed that we love those who brought us into the world and nurtured us. In the Bible one of the ten commandments given to Moses was 'Honour your Mother and your Father'. The recognition and respect of parents is mentioned in the Quran no less than 11 times. In Hindu families it is a common custom to bow down to touch the feet of elders and parents. Even in the secular world we talk easily of 'the love of a child for its mother' as though it were a given fact. Indeed, as children most of us who are brought up in a loving family do love our parents in an unconditional way. However, people grow up. As we mature we make the (sometimes unwelcome) discovery that our parents are people like any others with faults and unpleasant characteristics as well as strengths and virtues. We become adults and in time we may grow to dislike our parents but we are still bound to them by the ties of family. An uneasy relationship may be maintained by keeping our parents at a distance. They, too, may dislike the adult who has developed from the infant they nurtured. This kind of dislike between parents and children is seldom acknowledged in society.

It is generally taken for granted that elderly parents will be supported by their children, not necessarily financially but emotionally and practically. Care home staff show open disapproval of children who do not visit aging parents. Neighbours of elderly people comment on how often (or seldom) the children visit. If you have had an uneasy relationship with one or both parents you may have found it very difficult to help them when they became frail or ill or were hospitalized, but it is unlikely that you will have ignored them and refused to help. Society expects children to take care of their parents. The death of a parent often brings unpleasant feelings to the surface. We may not feel particularly sorry for the death if we have not really cared for a parent in life. Nevertheless, the feeling most likely to surface is that of guilt; guilt at having been unable to feel filial love, guilt at not having spent time with them, guilt at not visiting often enough or not expressing our love for them when we still could.

How can we deal with this kind of guilt? Pragmatic, exceptionally well-balanced people may be able to come to terms with their feelings, recognize them and put them aside. Others may never even acknowledge these feelings, carrying them through life until their sour memories and guilt turn to hatred.

Actually, as I grew up I became more and more estranged from my mother. I really came to dislike her. After I left home I had as little to do with her as possible. My two brothers didn't have this feeling of dislike but when my mother began to suffer from Alzheimer's disease the whole family seemed to expect me to be the one to support her (my father had died a year before) rather than either of them. I really resented that and as her behaviour became more and more difficult I was unable to feel any compassion or sympathy for her. I didn't actually mistreat her but I was glad when the time came for her to go into a care home and I visited as little as possible. After she died my initial feelings of relief were followed by massive feelings of guilt at not having been able to feel love in her lifetime.

Some people may find that these feelings of guilt at not retaining the unconditional love for our parent needs psychological therapy in order to allow a 'coming to terms' with the weight of guilt. Others may be able to address such feelings by talking them through with close friends and family. A great deal of unofficial 'therapy' happens between friends and family in private. Or perhaps we may be able to assuage guilt feelings by some actions following the death. Those with religious feelings may find solace in prayer and confession. Others may work through their guilt feelings in a practical way by, for example, using a part of any inheritance to help others, or by undertaking some charitable work of which their parents would have approved. Still others find comfort in raising a memorial. A splendid gravestone can give solace and assuage guilt for some; a tangible memorial or a service of remembrance can help others.

Guilt and blame

What we should try not to allow is the transference of guilt into blame. It is too easy to bury our own guilt feelings in blaming others; so easy that we may not even realize we are doing it. Consider the following:

'Well, if she hadn't been so difficult I would have visited Mum more often.'

'I would have looked after my father at home if my sister had not interfered.'

'My wife made my life so difficult – it was no wonder I neglected her.'

Any of these statements might be true and any of them might count in law as mitigating circumstances. However, if we are to use the analogy of the law then none of these mitigating circumstances would make the wrong-doing right. If I feel guilty because I consider that I neglected my dying mother in her last days than the fact that my sister's interference made the relationship so difficult that I opted out of caring doesn't make that neglect right. What such a fact might do is provide a reason for the neglect. I may still feel guilty because of what I failed to do, but the neglect is not my sister's fault. She is not to blame for my guilt. My guilt is my own. Understanding the reason for my neglect and accepting the guilt can be helpful.

The Catholic church has an interesting approach to guilt and wrong-doing: one is urged to acknowledge and accept the guilt and also urged to seek forgiveness. Then one's guilt is 'absolved', it is wiped clean. There is also an element of 'making good' the wrong-doing. Whilst not advocating a religious form of confession we might consider accepting that we were guilty of neglect if it were so. We can forgive ourselves in the knowledge that none of us are perfect. At the time of trial anyone could be found wanting. We can resolve to do better another time. If it helps, we can channel our guilt into doing good. Perhaps we might do some voluntary work with the sick and elderly or help in a hospice. However, such reparation is only one way to assuage guilt and not necessarily the best or most certain way. The most important thing is the acknowledgement and the forgiveness of self.

Guilty feelings

A common cause of guilt concerns broken promises referring to care. Older people aware of their failing health often put pressure on their families.

My mother made us all promise that we would not put her into a home. She used to make a huge point of getting us all to make a solemn promise about this and my brother and sisters and I all agreed that it would never happen. It was a stupid promise because although we could have managed between us if she had simply become frail we just could not cope when she developed progressive dementia. None of us could handle the physical moving and lifting nor the incontinence, and we did all try. For the last months of her life a care home was the only option and she was well looked after. But the guilt stayed with us for years, long after she died.

This kind of promise is often extracted from loving relatives and it is hard to resist when a loving parent or perhaps a partner is pleading with us to ensure they spend their last days in their own home. It can seem unbelievably cruel to refuse to make such a promise. Of course what we should do is assure the questioner that we will always care for them, that we will keep their interests at heart and that wherever possible no decisions about care will be made without consulting them. Refusing to make a promise about future care may cause us to suffer guilt but most of us would suffer from a far greater feeling of guilt over a promise made which we were later unable to keep.

If this is the situation you are in, you may feel not only guilty that you were unable to keep your promise but also ready to blame others for making it impossible to do so.

It is easy to fall into a pattern of 'if only':

'If only my sister had helped more we could have kept mum at home.'

'If only my husband had cooperated with the doctors he wouldn't have died before I could get to the hospital.'

These kinds of destructive thoughts may circulate in our brain constantly, even though we may be able to see that they are not helpful and probably not even true.

Sometimes people need professional counselling to accept that blaming others does not remove the guilt feelings. Some people can work through these feelings themselves. Perhaps one of the most important things is to understand that feelings of guilt are natural and so common as to be almost 'normal'.

My father had Alzheimer's for many years and was at end of his life. The consultant asked me whether I wanted to give him 'one last chance' and allow a PEG to be inserted (placing a tube directly into the stomach to allow liquid nutrition). I suppose it was the way that the consultant put it but of course I agreed. In retrospect I was only extending a life that had no quality and goodness knows if, or how much, he was suffering. I have regretted that decision every day since. I should have asked 'One more chance at what?' but of course when put in that position you don't, do you?

Many of us are familiar with the guilt arising from having left things too late. Someone has died and now it is too late to make peace about that stupid argument, that missed visit; too late to apologize for that thoughtless remark; too late to just say that you really do love them. As mentioned previously, the finality of death seems to take us all aback. It can be really difficult just to acknowledge that we cannot now put things right with the person who has died. Some people find that arranging the funeral or the memorial service helps with such feelings. This may be one reason why feelings can run so high in families on the subject of 'getting things right' for the funeral and why arguments can break out so easily over 'what he would have wanted'. Others find that arranging a memorial such as a headstone on a grave, an entry in a book of remembrance or a donation to charity can help to assuage the guilt of having left it too late to make amends. Some people have found that writing a letter to the deceased asking for forgiveness can help. Of course the letter will never be received but the act of writing it can truly help. Another idea is to do something special for another family member – perhaps the widow or the child of the deceased – in their memory.

Some of us may have found it difficult to express our love verbally and will suffer guilt due to that lack of expression. Perhaps in such a case we might examine whether, despite not putting our feelings into words, we actually did express our love by our actions. If you helped your parent when they needed it (maybe you did their shopping or helped fix the car or managed their money for them) or visited them at home or in hospital or care home, if you 'fought their corner' with officialdom or with medical staff, then you showed that you cared. Words can come easily and actions may show our feelings in a different and better way.

A surprisingly common cause of guilt feelings is simply the act of survival. People who survived disasters in which several others died commonly suffer from depression and feelings of guilt because they survived when others did not. In a similar way it is possible to feel guilt as well as sorrow, and also relief and even gratitude, if, say, you are the survivor of a car crash in which someone you loved died. You may spend hours asking yourself why you were 'chosen' to survive. Religious people may constantly ask God why He allowed them to survive and not a loved one. A parent of a child who has died, especially, may feel intense guilt because they feel that they should have been the one to die because it is surely the duty of a parent to protect their child, even to the extent of dying in their place.

Some good can result from survivor guilt. Properly addressed it can help people find meaning and make sense out of an otherwise horrific experience. It may actually help the survivor to cope with the helplessness and powerlessness of being in a life-threatening situation without the power or ability to protect or save others. This kind of guilt can also be one way to express a connection to those who have died, so that, for a time, it becomes a way of keeping them alive.

Survival guilt is commonly associated with post-traumatic stress disorder and is often best treated professionally. However, you can help yourself by acknowledging the guilt. Whether you *should* feel guilty is not the point, if you actually do feel guilty. So accept that you feel guilty.

Moving on

Some people find that helping others in the same situation can assist in coping with the guilt, but others find this is the very worst thing for them. You should not feel that you have to get involved in helping with rehabilitation schemes unless you feel strongly motivated to do so. But there is no reason why, with help from others, you should not seek your own way of dealing with your feelings. This will allow you to come out at the other end of the long tunnel of guilt. For some people this may involve 'talking therapy', either formal and professional or informal with helpful friends. For others this may involve taking some action or actions which may have a connection with the cause of the guilt.

Feelings of guilt may manifest in many ways. Guilt does not always make us feel depressed and outwardly miserable. Guilt can manifest as spite against others perceived as more fortunate ('Easy to be good tempered when you have never had any troubles') or perceived as equally unfortunate ('I coped, so why can't they?'). Feelings of guilt may result in unjust accusations or family conflict. Occasionally guilt may manifest as a complete lack of interest in others' troubles or others' good fortune.

After my wife died I found myself frequently dwelling on disagreements which we'd had in the past or on times when I had felt she hadn't supported me. I began to believe that she had been a bad partner and that our marriage had not been happy. It was as if our 20 years together had been a time of difficulty and despair. In actual fact we had been very happily married. Gradually it dawned on me that I was coping with both guilt and unhappiness by making her the scapegoat – that by talking myself into believing that we had been unhappy and that she had been a 'bad' wife I was attempting to come to terms with this ghastly happening. One day my son pointed out that I was putting a totally untrue slant on one particular event from the past and that helped me to begin to turn my feelings around and to accept reality. It didn't all come right straight away but I can date my acceptance of her death from that day.

Feelings of guilt can wreck any new relationship. Family members may resent or feel unable to accept a new partner or relationship. This is especially common with children from a previous marriage, however physically adult they may be. Their loyalty remains to the person who has died and some will refuse to accept or allow their parent to move on with another partner, causing the parent to feel guilt even whilst they are finding new happiness. Families may also feel a sense of guilt if they accept the new relationship, as though they are betraying the person who has died. These emotions are very complex and distressing. The truth is that someone who has spent most of their adult life in a long-term relationship may well find living alone very difficult and will perhaps look for another partner to share their life with. This is not dismissing or demeaning to the relationship they have had, but fulfilling a need to love and be loved, a very natural human condition. Feelings of guilt may be natural, but families in this situation should try to remain compassionate. It is a compliment to a past relationship rather than a betrayal that someone left alone should try to re-create that feeling of love and closeness. Open conversations will help the acceptance of this human need and allow the bereaved partner to have a new and fulfilling relationship and families to let their kinder feelings surface.

> It took me so long to accept the fact that my father wanted to marry again. My mother's death from breast cancer had been so traumatic that I felt he should be grieving long after others had accepted he could move on. When he introduced me to his new 'girl-friend' I was polite but inside I was seething. She seemed shallow and stupid compared to my mother and I couldn't see why he seemed to feel such pleasure in her company. He knew how I felt and I am ashamed to think now of the way I refused to let him talk to me about it. To be honest I still don't find her company interesting or entertaining but I have come to realize that he is happy with her and I am able to be glad that he has found new happiness (even whilst I resent it).

Feelings of guilt seem to be a part of the grieving process and it is sensible to understand and accept this. If you feel (or your friends and relations suggest) that your guilt feelings are excessive then it may be time to look for professional counselling to help you work through the reasons for this. Above all, it is important to try not to feel guilty about feeling guilty!

If you are a friend, relative or other supporter of someone who is bereaved and you are aware of their guilt feelings you may wonder what you can do to help. Try to avoid such phrases as:

'You shouldn't feel guilty' (they may then feel guilty at feeling guilty).

'You did all you could' (perhaps their guilt is because they feel they did not do all they could).

'It's time to get over it.'

'It is X who should feel guilty, not you.'

Probably the most supportive thing you can do is to listen to the bereaved even if they are going over things again and again. Talking therapy really does seem to work. It may help to put another point of view, but never do this as an argument or an 'answer'. You might say:

'I wonder what more you could have done.'

'Do you wish you had had the chance to tell her you loved her/to say goodbye?'

'You were under such stress at the time.'

'It's hard not to feel guilt. I remember how guilty I felt when…'

You can suggest professional counselling if you feel this is appropriate, but remember that grief and guilt do not have a time limit. You do not know when it is time for someone to move on or to forget their guilt or accept their feelings. Your support and your ability to listen and to be there is of immense value. If your suggestions of professional help are rejected, this is not a rejection of you. You can tailor your support to the amount of time and the type of activity you feel able to give. Try especially not to feel guilty yourself. Any support you give can be helpful, but we all have our own limits and lives to lead.

Chapter 4

More About Grief

Much has been written about grief, and theories abound. A search via the internet will bring up:

- the six stages of Dr Eric Lindemann (1944)
- the five stages of Elizabeth Kübler-Ross (1969)
- the four stages of Worden or Sidney Zisook (2009; 1987, 1993)
- the three stages of Dr Roberta Temes and Geoffrey Gorer (1992; 1967).

These are well-known theories, and you would find plenty more if you were to continue your search including the theory that there aren't any stages at all but an assortment of feelings that arise! However, theories are simply that; they are different people's opinions.

So much for theories but what are the facts? The *fact* is that grief is potentially the worst emotional pain any of us may suffer. The fact is also that most of us survive our grief and over a period of time we will start to feel better.

No one wants to hear the old chestnut that 'time heals all wounds' and this book is not about such platitudes. Grief has been likened to a journey. We never know when that journey is going to begin, and we don't know how long it will take. There is no 'route planner' for this journey but it is likely that at the end of it you will be a very different person from the one you were before you started. The experience of grieving will change you.

No one wants to think about death in advance. People resist making a will, refuse to write an advance directive, don't want to plan their funeral and sometimes even resist actions which, whilst not necessarily connected with death, make it seem nearer – actions like making a power of attorney, for example.

It is inconceivable to most of us that we may go out to work today and not come back, and we certainly don't often consider that one of our family members or friends may do the same. When we do consider it (perhaps in a moment of philosophical conversation or due to the sudden death of someone we know) we may discuss it, may even resolve to carry out some actions like those outlined above, but often we quickly move on from these thoughts.

Nothing in our lives prepares us for end of life. Death usually comes as a complete shock to those left behind. It seems just not possible. In fact, the first reaction to news of death is usually disbelief. It does not seem logical that one moment someone is there and the next minute they are not, almost like a perverse magic trick.

Even when death is 'expected' after a long illness or very late in life, you still hear people say, 'We knew he was going to die but it was such a shock when it happened.'

Logic may indicate that someone is going to die but the emotion we feel when they actually die has nothing to do with logic.

Stages of grief

Some people benefit from understanding that grief has stages. It can be helpful to understand that you are not going mad, to know that others have suffered and survived and moved on with their lives. This knowledge can be of help and get you through the darkest hours.

The stages that Elizabeth Kübler-Ross identified in the late 1960s are arguably still one of the more popular theories of grieving and are often quoted in relation to the grieving process for those left behind. Her theories were first published in 1969 in her book *On Death and Dying* which became an international best seller (Simon & Schuster, 1969). Elizabeth identified some stages of grief and recognized these when she was working with people who had a diagnosis of a terminal illness and who were in fact grieving for the loss of their own lives. They are:

- denial
- anger
- guilt
- depression, and
- acceptance

and they have been adopted as stages for those grieving for the loss of others.

Denial is often considered to be the mind's defence mechanism. If the consequences of the news of death were to be realized in the one moment of receiving the news, the mind might not be able to cope. Denial is almost like a net that catches the bad news and allows it to slowly sieve through to the conscious mind. Receiving extremely good news (like winning the lottery) can cause the same reaction of disbelief and denial.

Anger often follows denial – anger with the person who died, with the doctor, with the messenger, with God or even with yourself. It may seem strange to think that you might feel angry with the person who has died, but it is common.

Blaming medical staff or mistakes made during treatment is also a common form of anger and often understandable. This (together with the possibility of litigation) may be the reason why doctors feel so unable to say that they are sorry when things have gone wrong.

> When my husband died it was partially because one member of the medical team had 'forgotten' to give the right medication. In fact, even with the medication he probably would only have lived a few more days but no one would admit the fault. I didn't want to sue anyone. It would have helped if someone could just have said, 'I am sorry, there was a mistake.'

Guilt is another very common emotion after death. As Elizabeth Kübler-Ross said: 'Guilt is perhaps the most painful companion of death' (1969, p.169). It is a very natural emotion and we have devoted a whole chapter to it in this book (see Chapter 3 Grief and Guilt).

Depression is arguably the most dangerous stage in the grieving process. Not everyone experiences depression to any significant degree, but some level of 'what is the point of life?' attitude is often experienced. Some people find it very difficult to come out of the depression, especially if they have a previous history of depressive illness or if they have had multiple losses throughout their lives or are elderly and feel they have very little to look forward to.

Acceptance is relative. Accepting does not mean forgetting but the constant wish for things to be as they once were can be replaced by a search for new relationships and new activities. A sense of longing may re-surface from time to time for years and this should be expected

More recently Sidney Zisook describes four stages: Separation Distress: this is a soup of feelings like sadness, anxiety, pain, helplessness, anger, shame, yearning and loneliness. Traumatic Distress: this includes states of disbelief and shock, intrusions, and efforts to avoid intrusions and the spike of emotions they produce; guilt, remorse, and regrets and social withdrawal (Zisook 1987; Zisook and Schuchter 1993).

J. William Worden highlights four tasks: to accept the reality of the loss, to process the pain of grief, to adjust to a world without the deceased, and to find an enduring connection with the deceased in the midst of embarking on a new life (2009).

In his book Dr. Phil feels that there are possibly no stages at all but 'but an array of feelings that arise' (McGraw 2008, p.70).

The 'downside' to the broad acceptance of any stages of grief is that sometimes others can expect you to be 'at a different stage by now'. There is little tolerance for someone who after months or even years is still saying 'I still find it hard to believe', for example. The attitude tends to be, 'Shouldn't you have moved on by now?' It is wrong to expect someone to move rapidly through the different stages or even to assume that everyone will experience all the stages in any particular order or at all. We are a very impatient society, perhaps partly thanks to the internet. We expect everything right now and the thought of supporting someone through a long journey of grief can make the most patient person want to move it along.

> My mother died when I was 16. No one in my family spoke about her illness or subsequent death and I locked up all the emotions inside me, the pain was so intense that I was afraid of opening myself up to it. It wasn't until the 30th anniversary of her death when I was in my mid-40s that I realized that I had to face it and started to have intensive bereavement therapy. I couldn't tell anyone because I knew they would be amazed that I was still deeply suffering with my loss 30 years later.

Changes after bereavement

Bereavement can be complicated by all the changes that occur. When a partner dies, he or she may have fulfilled many roles and the loss of each role will elicit a feeling of grief. Those whose lives were intertwined like roots of two trees will feel as though they have to go through a process of finding which were their own roots and rebuilding their lives, which can be very frightening. No longer do they have the support of their partner and the world looks like a very different place now that they are alone. The whole landscape of life has changed in an instant; some friendships will also change and many newly single people find that their 'couple friends' melt away.

Conversations and comments

Attitudes concerning conversations around the death are still in the dark ages and, perversely, the well-intentioned comments or lack of comments from other people can make grieving harder. There's an extraordinarily illogical belief that some people have (even, bizarrely, at the funeral) that if you don't talk about the person who has died the mourning family member won't think about them. 'I didn't want to upset her by talking about him' is quite a common comment.

Some of my husband's colleagues came over to see me shortly after the funeral. They stayed for over an hour and didn't mention my husband once!! When they left I felt utterly depressed, it was as though the 20 years they worked with my husband had meant nothing. I know that wasn't a logical feeling but nevertheless it is how I felt. I think they believed that if they didn't mention him I wouldn't think about him or that if they mentioned him I would get upset. Yes, I was upset my husband had died but they made me feel worse and I didn't think that was possible.

To behave in an abnormal way is normal in abnormal circumstances. This is a sentence that you can write down and pin up. Everything you do and feel under these trying circumstances is normal, including:

- crying a lot, often at most inopportune moments
- wanting to talk about what happened over and over again
- thinking that everyone else's life seems to have moved on except yours
- realizing that the death is old news to everyone else but you
- feeling very alone
- thinking that you see the person who has died or can feel them or smell them
- dreaming about the person who has died and feeling sure that you have (in some strange alternative reality) met and conversed with them
- not wanting to get up/washed/dressed
- waking up very early in the morning

- forgetting upon waking that the person you are mourning is dead
- finding it very hard to sleep at night
- feeling fine one moment and a complete mess the next
- going through a lot of 'if only' and 'what if' and 'I wish I had/hadn't'
- finding yourself thinking 'this time last week/month/year'.

If someone tells you that you should have moved to a different stage you can tell them that grief has its own time frame and moves at its own pace and then change the subject. It is very important to have someone to talk to about how you feel, but it doesn't always have to be the same person. By talking to different people at different times you avoid overwhelming any one person with your pain. You could call Samaritans or the Cruse Bereavement Care helpline and tell them how you are feeling from time to time if you feel that your friends are being overburdened by your grief. However close the friendship, you don't want to impose on the goodwill of others. Samaritans are not only for those who are about to take their life but also for those in deep emotional distress – and that may well be you.

Talking to the person who died, or writing to them, is also quite cathartic and may help to release the emotions. You can talk to them about how you are feeling, write to them, share memories with them. This doesn't guarantee you a one-way ticket to a padded cell – one of the more popular recent theories of grief is 'continuing bonds', which suggests that it is healthy to continue to have a relationship with the person that has died.

> When my mother died, I wrote her a letter. I made an appointment at the undertakers to spend some time alone with her. I read out the letter and then put it next to her. As I left I kissed her. It felt very personal and intimate and helped me to come to terms with the ending of her life by saying goodbye.

You cannot be expected to cut the relationship off abruptly and you don't have to do that. You can't be expected to have a relationship that spans a significant period of time and then just switch it off because they are no longer alive. This is not realistic. Don't tell yourself that you are strange because you continue to communicate with them. This is more common than you know. You can continue to have a relationship with them, continue to talk to them, and share your feelings. Loneliness is a terrible thing and perhaps keeping the person close to you in some way will alleviate that feeling. They may not still be physically present but the emotional ties still exist.

> Graham was away quite a lot of the time so texting became our main way of communicating. He used to text me every morning to say good morning, throughout the day if something happened that amused him, and every evening to say goodnight. He died very suddenly – it was a terrible shock and I missed him dreadfully. For many months I found myself texting him daily. I didn't want to let go of him and I felt by still texting him he would remain a part of my life. I wouldn't have to say goodbye. Over a year has passed and I still miss him and still send him the occasional text, but not as frequently as I did.

One way to understand the almost physical pain of grief is to think of the attachments that grow between people as physical but invisible. You might try to imagine that, as you slowly grow attached to people, an invisible thread grows between the two of you that attaches itself to the heart, and that when the relationship is past its sell-by date, the attachment withers and drops off. In this scenario when someone dies it is as though the thread between you is suddenly wrenched out of the heart, leaving a gaping raw wound. Over a period of time the wound starts to slowly heal so the pain isn't as raw as it was, but it is still very sore. The wound will always remain sensitive but not feel as raw as the period after the initial wrench.

My mother died of cancer when I was 18. I followed in her footsteps becoming a ballet teacher. My relationship with my two children I think is much closer because of losing her and my husband often complains that I put the children first. It's as though I want to make up for the loss of my relationship with my mother by being closer to my children. In many ways her death has really influenced our entire family dynamics.

Grief doesn't have an end date or a sell-by date – it can be ongoing for many years. The loss of a significant other, whether it is a mother, father, husband, wife or child, is an ongoing loss that changes shape according to the stage of our life in which that person is missed. The loss of a mother or father can still be keenly felt 20, 30 or 40 years later, at a time when you may most need that person in your life. For example, at the birth of a first child or grandchild people often feel again the loss of a parent. At a significant wedding, the absence of a partner may be most keenly felt and unless you have someone who shared that relationship it can be a very lonely time. Grief is an ongoing process but most people will forget that and expect you to have moved on.

> When my son was killed in a motorbike accident you won't believe how many women said to me, 'If anything happened to my son I would die!'
>
> What did they mean by that? That they loved their sons more than I loved mine? That if I had loved my son more I would have killed myself? Was that comment meant to be helpful?!

There are many factors that can complicate grief. One way to explain that is to think of water flowing from the kitchen sink. As we go through life we experience different losses, and those losses can be compared to the water that pours down the sink. Loss is natural. We cannot go through life without saying goodbye in different ways to different people – those who move away, those who leave us at the end of a relationship and of course those who die. All these losses should be able to flow naturally down the sink. However, if one of those losses isn't processed or is not properly experienced it will block the sink and any future losses will not be able to flow through. So the grief will build up until it overflows. This overflow represents a complicated grieving process that needs professional counselling, and such a process will often identify the original blockage.

My father was a long-distance lorry driver. I adored him. During the school holidays I joined him in the cab of his lorry. He was killed whilst driving in Germany. I was used to him being away and told myself that he was still away driving.

That was 25 years ago. In the meanwhile my mother died of a broken heart, though cancer was the diagnosis. I am still actively grieving for my mother although 20 years have passed. It wasn't until someone told me the blocked sink theory that I realized that my father's death was the blockage in the pipe and my mother's death filled the sink and was still overflowing into my life.

Grief after someone dies after a long illness or dementia

If you have been caring for someone who is suffering from a protracted illness or dementia and they subsequently die, you need to mourn in the same way as you would for any other person.

Grief doesn't take a different route just because the person deteriorated over a long period either physically or mentally or both. You are entitled to feel as much sorrow, as much anger and as much depression as anyone else who is mourning. You should not allow anyone to persuade you otherwise.

The fact that you may feel relief that your caring duties have ended can seem to be a reason to feel guilty. The gap left by not physically caring for and not visiting the person who has died is as real as the gap left by any other death. The need for a service of remembrance or to celebrate a life now extinguished is just as important. As time passes it becomes easier to remember the days before, and to recall the life and the person you once knew and perhaps, at last, you might find it possible to see the days when they had dementia/were seriously ill as just another chapter in their life and even to find some meaning in what then seemed a terrible blow.

When someone begins to suffer the effects of dementia or any other progressive illness, it is not just they who are affected. The effects are felt by everyone around them. Many people describe living with someone with dementia or some terminal illnesses as a prolonged period of mourning. Slowly it seems that you lose the person whom you used to know and love. Bit by bit the things you love about them are lost. They may cease to empathize with you, seem to cease to care about you. Conversations you used to enjoy no longer happen. Things you used to enjoy doing together are no longer possible or no longer give pleasure. After a while the act of caring overcomes the act of sharing. You become the carer and no longer the wife, husband, son or daughter.

When someone who has been suffering for a long time dies, then often those offering consolation want to suggest that death in such cases is 'a blessing' or 'a relief' for those left behind. It isn't always easy for those close to the person to see it this way.

Maybe you do not find it a blessing or a relief. Grief has many facets. Whilst it is true that you may be able to acknowledge that you (or they) would not have wanted life to continue if it is no longer life but simply existence, something within you still wants back the person who has died. The grief may be unfathomable to others but it is nevertheless there. Other people may believe that because you 'lost' the person to dementia or cancer long ago there is now no real reason to grieve, and that the person who has died is no longer suffering. This is a very logical reasoning, but as we mentioned previously grief has nothing to do with logic. Grief is an emotion.

The fact is that all the time the person you loved was physically alive they were with you. They may perhaps have lost the ability to share, to converse, to give comfort or to empathize but they were still physically alive, still needed you, still, actually, gave you something to live for. Most carers can relate how much the person for whom they cared filled up their life. Needing almost constant attention whilst they still lived at home, and even if they later moved to a care home or hospital, their needs filled up the life of the carer. Visits are planned and timetabled; their needs are uppermost in the mind when the carer goes shopping. Even trips away have to be meticulously planned. Festivals and celebrations have to include extra planning: When on Christmas Day will a visit take place? Shall we bring home the person who is ill for a birthday celebration? Should they be included in a wedding ceremony? The needs of the person with dementia or a terminal illness have to be considered along with the needs of other family and friends.

The journey of grief is a solitary one. Although we have no choice but to walk it alone, this is a period of time in our lives when we need to access as much support from the community as possible, and yet paradoxically at this time our emotional energy is at its lowest, and we are least able to reach out and ask for the help that we so badly need.

One of the barriers to a healthy grieving process is caused by the disappearance of any external symbol of mourning. In the past, someone who was in mourning was easily recognized. The end of the tradition of wearing black, or a black armband, has meant that those in mourning no longer have an external sign of their internal emotional state. No one knows that we need to be treated with care. These external signs of grief were almost like a 'handle with care' sticker. Now there is no obvious way for their grief to be announced to those who do not know them and an unhappy mourner is more likely to be considered as just having woken up feeling irritable than to be grieving.

It is for this reason that we strongly advocate the return of an external symbol to allow the mourner to make known that they have suffered a loss without having to make an embarrassing announcement that most would shy away from doing.

We suggest the symbol of the leaf, which has no religious or cultural significance, and yet, at the same time, holds a universal symbolic significance (relating to the tree of life, the eternal changing of the seasons, nature, varying seasonal colours, falling autumnal and winter leaves, absorption back to the soil signifying the circle of life, etc.). We chose a deep purple colour to distinguish it from (perhaps) a leaf worn as an ordinary brooch. It has an easily recognizable connection to nature, the ultimate circle of life. It can be bought from our website.

Coping with bereavement

The old adage does have some truth – when you are bereaved things do get better over time. We may feel worse on some days before we start to feel better, but time does make a difference. There will be a day when you wake up in the morning and find that your loss is not the first thing you think about and you will get through a whole day without crying. There is also some truth in the suggestion that it helps to keep busy.

When my daughter died it was with tremendous effort that I motivated myself to do stuff – I joined a new social group, I restarted an old hobby – I kept active – I saw friends. I read a lot of books and I learned not to shy away from the subject of bereavement. I now feel at ease talking about my loss, but it took time. None of this took away the enduring pain of grief but it did take the edge off it.

If you have a job which you enjoy, take the opportunity to get back to working life as soon as you feel able. If you hate your job then perhaps use this life-changing event as an excuse to re-think your working life.

In our book *End of Life: The Essential Guide to Caring* we recommend considering the benefits of volunteering. If you do not need to take paid employment and decide not to do so, do consider this. Any positive activity that gets you out of the house and into a wider social network has got to be worth considering and we believe that human beings are cleverly wired to get huge benefits out of giving to others. In general, volunteers report that they get much more out of volunteering than they put in:

> Over the past two decades we have seen a growing body of research that indicates volunteering provides individual health benefits in addition to social benefits. This research has established a strong relationship between volunteering and health: those who volunteer have lower mortality rates, greater functional ability, and lower rates of depression later in life than those who do not volunteer. Comparisons of the health benefits of volunteering for different age groups have also shown that older volunteers are the most likely to receive greater benefits from volunteering, whether because they are more likely to face higher incidence of illness or because volunteering provides them with physical and social activity and a sense of purpose at a time when their social roles are changing. Some of these findings also indicate that volunteers who devote a 'considerable' amount of time to volunteer activities (about 100 hours per year) are most likely to exhibit positive health outcomes.
>
> (Corporation for National and
> Community Service 2007)

Volunteer activities can strengthen social ties and forge new ones. The experience of helping others leads to a sense of greater self-worth and trust. It isn't just about 'doing good' but more about feeling of use to others, having to think about something other than your loss, not letting people down and being valued for the vital role you play. So, if you are not in paid employment we urge you strongly to consider volunteering – even if only for a few hours each week. If you don't know where you can be of most use and your inclination doesn't lead you into a particular area than there are local Volunteer Bureaux who will be only too happy to discuss your strengths and abilities and point you to a volunteer post which suits you.

Many people who are grieving find that owning a pet can be a real life-line. There are rescue pets of varying ages and sizes with numerous built-in benefits looking for a home, and their unconditional love will never be more welcome than at this time. Again there is some evidence that these benefits are based in fact and are not the fantasies of besotted animal lovers. The presence of a companion animal on the grief experiences of 89 newly widowed Caucasian women was explored by Dr Sharon E. Brolin (1987). She worked with 55 non-pet owners and 34 bonded dog owners. Her findings indicated that the widows who were bonded to their dogs experienced significantly fewer of the feelings of despair that accompany grief than the non-pet owners. In addition, providing that they were in good health prior to their spouse's death, they remained in good health, compared with the non-pet owners who noted deterioration in their health after the bereavement. Brolin suggests that the comfort and nurturing (similar to the direct effects noted by McNicholas *et al.* 2005) that the pet provides has 'mediating and therapeutic effect on the health of the widow'. She also notes that family members 'should not assume that the pet is a burden to the widow... Families might unwittingly remove a source of strength and comfort...' (Brolin cited in Hardiman 2010, pp.15–16).

If you are mobile, any dog will also force you to leave the solitude of your home to go 'walkies' and whilst out you may well find yourself chatting to other dog owners. Mutual interests are an easy way to meet new people. Any exercise is better than none, and exercise is a proven antidote to depression. Of course, owning a dog is a huge responsibility and if you don't feel able to commit yourself, perhaps look at the possibility of walking a neighbour's pet or assisting someone who has a dog, and is less mobile, to keep their pet. In the UK, the Cinnamon Trust will have details of anyone in your area who is either ill or incapacitated and in need of a dog walker.

Perhaps think of grief as like the sea. Incomparably deep in some places, and quite shallow in others, some days so stormy you fear you could drown in it, and other days so calm you feel you can float through it.

And like the sea it can change suddenly from calm to stormy and back again.

When one of my closest friends and both of my parents died within a very short time, I was devastated. Roxy, my beautiful Kooikerhondje became my constant source of comfort, my reason for getting up and carrying on each day. Because she needed to be walked, fed and played with, I was soon back into my routine and soon interacting with other dog walkers...who became my friends. Normality returned to my life. Her excitement when I returned home was joyous and reminded me of the pleasure life still held. She had shared time with my friend and my parents and I had lots of happy memories and photos of those times. She was a link to those people and that link was so important in helping me to grieve and to carry on.

On the journey of grief each of us will take a different route. Each will choose our own landmarks. We will travel at our own unique speed and will navigate using the tools provided by our culture, experience and faith. In the end, we will be forever changed by our journey.

Chapter 5

Families in Conflict

The word 'family' has a cosy sound. We talk of 'friends and family'. We say that someone is treated 'like family'. Things that we know are called 'familiar'.

Most of us would like to think that when things get difficult our family will help us, will stand by us, will believe in us. At difficult times we like to believe that our family will support us – and what time could be more difficult than a time of bereavement?

The sad fact is that the time of bereavement is an emotional time. It is a time when most of us suffer from mixed feelings – sorrow yes, the most obvious emotion, but also perhaps relief, shame, guilt distress, anger and bewilderment.

When Gallup International Institute carried out a national survey in 1997 on 'Spiritual beliefs and the dying process' (George 1997), the key spiritual concerns mentioned by people questioned were:

- not being forgiven by someone for something they had done

- not having a blessing from a family member or religious advisor.

When considering questions about life after death the reassurances that gave people the most comfort related to these concerns:

- desire for reconciliation with those they had hurt, or who had hurt them
- the belief that death is not the end, but a passage.

In both these crucial areas, not being forgiven and a desire for reconciliation were key concerns for those dying. Conflict with family and friends can cause endless upset during our lives and an uneasy passage into end of life.

Usually our loved ones want to rally around at such a time. People want to be useful and to feel that they are helping. Helping someone else in their grief can help one to come to terms with the grief that we too are suffering. Adult children who take the burden of registering the death or organizing the funeral arrangements for a parent not only feel useful and caring but their actions are helping to get them through this ghastly time of trial. Distant relatives who make contact, send messages, cards and letters, and attend the funeral not only reassure the widow or widower that their partner is remembered but their very attentiveness helps them in their sorrow and perhaps in their guilt if they feel they should have kept in touch more.

But emotional times bring to the surface hidden emotions, feelings which may have been suppressed, resentments fuelled by guilt or by long-past events; and these emotions have a habit of being vent at the most awkward moments. In our book *End of Life: The Essential Guide to Caring* we discussed in some detail the difficult moments that arise in families in the first days after bereavement and at funerals. It is worth briefly looking at these now:

- When someone has died, those closest to them are in a state of shock. They may find it very difficult to respond even to sympathetic queries or expressions of condolence. It is good to understand this and not to take offence if our well-meant expressions of sympathy are not met with polite replies.

- Contradictory feelings and emotions are not easily laid to rest. People are also often grieving for the good relationship they either lost or did not have. Their grief is complicated by the fact that they will not now ever be able to 'make peace'. They may feel immensely guilty that they were not able to give the person who has died the right support at the end of life.

- Post-funeral gatherings are an important part of the grieving process. They allow mourners to talk about the deceased, to share memories and to share sorrow, and this also gives the immediate family an opportunity to communicate their pain with others who also are feeling the loss.

- Feelings run very high at this emotional time and it is not unknown for major feuds to have their beginnings in a perceived slight at the funeral.

(Jordan and Kauffman 2010, p.141)

> My brother made a rather thoughtless remark at the funeral of my sister's husband Mark. It wasn't a particularly nasty remark, just thoughtless and a bit critical. In any other circumstances it would probably have passed unnoticed. However, it caused a major row with Mark's mother, and my sister was left playing 'piggy in the middle' and trying to placate both sides. It took her years to forgive my brother properly for putting her in that situation. It was only an 'off the cuff' remark but the after-effects were out of all proportion.

In this book we are looking beyond the immediate period of mourning but it may be that you are having to deal with the effects of something which happened or which was said at the funeral or in the days immediately after death and which is still causing problems in the weeks, months or even years after that.

Putting things right

Often one finds that time, as in many other situations, will help to heal any breach. Many of us become more aware of how important the support of our family and friends is to us as we age. Sometimes age and the passage of time brings wisdom and the realization that certain things matter less than others. If you want to help this natural healing by passage of time then it is best to avoid any attempt to whip up emotion or revert to imagined slights or get into long discussions about seemingly aberrant behaviour at the funeral or in the early days of mourning. This may seem an obvious statement, but sometimes with the best of intentions it is believed that by allowing people to vent their feelings or to intensively discuss a thoughtless action/comment it is helping to 'clear the air'. This is seldom true. Naturally it would not be wise to refuse to talk about something which has caused great upset. Equally unhelpful is to maintain a tight-lipped 'let's not go there' attitude. Perhaps the best thing of all is to empathize but not dwell on a supposed wrong. Consider phrases such as:

'I understand how upset you must have been...' (keep it in the past).

'He must have been really distressed to put his foot in it like that' (his behaviour was wrong but he didn't mean it that way).

'I expect he feels bad about it now.'

'It was a dreadful time for us all.'

'It's lucky you are not someone to bear a grudge for things said in the heat of the moment.'

If time doesn't help to heal the hurt an apology can work wonders. Perhaps the person who said/did the hurtful thing realizes how they have 'upset the apple cart' and would be willing to say sorry. But perhaps they don't even realize they have caused any trouble at all. Family feuds and resentments often spring up due to a remark, an action, or lack of action which goes unnoticed by the person responsible. You often hear people say things like 'I don't understand why she avoids me now' or 'We used to be so close but now he never calls'. Often the speaker is genuinely in ignorance of the cause of the upset. Sometimes it can really help just to explain the facts if you know them – but make sure you really do know them.

My husband's brother and his wife and children had a habit of just turning up at his parents' house as the whim took them. One Christmas they just turned up on Christmas Day and it turned out to be such a happy visit that I know my mother-in-law hoped it would happen again in the same way. In fact the following Christmas they didn't come (nor had they intimated that they would) and at the end of the day she became very upset because they hadn't called. My father-in-law never forgave them for that but he also never explained why, and the entire family suffered a needless estrangement because of something which my brother-in-law not only didn't do but remained ignorant of his failure to do. I thought it was really weird and stupid but I didn't feel able to get involved in order to sort it out. Later, when my brother-in-law wasn't even invited to his father's funeral I wished I had said something.

It is often a good thing to remind ourselves of the fact that death is final. When death comes it is often, as the Bible is fond of reminding us, 'like a thief in the night' in a way and at a time that is so unexpected that we are totally shocked as well as bereft. We cannot make our excuses to someone after they have died, we cannot explain ourselves or beg for forgiveness. It is too late. How much better, then, to take the time to reconcile matters now? Perhaps we could ask ourselves exactly how important that chance remark was, how devastating that lack of a letter or card, how cruelly meant that omission. Conversely we might debate how difficult it might be to make the first contact, to ignore a supposed slight, to offer a hand in reconciliation. This is not meant to deny the hurt or unhappiness that may have been caused. It is a suggestion that we might like to put things right, to reconcile *before it is too late.*

Sometimes it really is difficult to approach someone in person. It might be found that a letter or a friendly card may open the way to reconciliation. Perhaps you don't need to mention the act or words which caused the upset. A family member may recognize a gesture for what it is and respond in kind.

The world is not perfect and nor are the people in it. It may be that efforts at reconciliation are rebuffed and you may feel that in making those efforts you have belittled your own sense of hurt. This is a hard emotion to deal with. It isn't always easy to feel that you have done the right thing if others reject you. However, if there is a genuine desire to make peace, a reconciliation is possible.

When offers are rejected

Why do people reject efforts at reconciling a wrong? There may be a number of reasons.

Others may feel so wronged that an apology or a 'reaching out' doesn't seem to be sufficient to right the sense of hurt. Some people find it very difficult indeed to accept an apology – certainly with any grace. A grudging acceptance may make things worse. Consider the following replies:

'Well, at least you know you were wrong.'

'Do you expect me to accept an apology just like that?'

'You may feel sorry now but it's too late.'

'What you did was unforgiveable.'

Replies and rejections like these can bounce the whole matter back into the realms of 'the unforgiveable wrong' and prevent any form of reconciliation.

I hadn't spoken to my sister-in-law for months. At my husband's mother's funeral she had accused us of not looking after her mother properly. We had borne the brunt of the day-to-day anxiety and care as my mother-in-law slowly deteriorated with Alzheimer's disease. My sister-in-law had visited only once a month and then at the funeral she came out with such hurtful accusations that I couldn't bear to speak to her afterwards. My husband was deeply hurt and refused to have any more to do with her. However, he became ill himself shortly afterwards and I remember waking up one night and realizing that if we weren't careful the whole unhappy scenario would be repeated at his funeral in the near future. So I sent her a card with just a short message saying that her brother was ill and would she like to visit. Luckily it did work and they were reconciled. Actually my husband didn't die from that illness and I was glad that he and his sister had a good relationship for years afterwards.

How you handle a rejection or grudging acceptance is perhaps a major indication of character. You might think that it would take a saint to agree with counter-accusations or replies such as those above. You might feel that you have stooped low enough in making the first effort at reconciliation. You may feel a hot rejoinder coming to your lips concerning where the fault lies. And so the situation lingers on, never being reconciled, never being closed.

Perhaps the best way around this kind of situation is to adopt a disinterested response. Keep your tone low and neutral and say something like:

'I was sure you would want to let bygones be bygones.'

'I'm glad to have been able to explain *before* it was too late.'

'I know you wouldn't wish to bear a grudge.'

'It would be nice if we could be on good terms again.'

Often after a painful discussion it may be realized that a comment or an action has been completely misunderstood. You may despair of the number of years spent in acrimony and wish you could turn back the time and have had this discussion at an earlier stage.

> After my mother died, my father seemed to adopt a divide and conquer attitude and he succeeded in causing a rift between my sister and I. We didn't contact each other at all for about ten years, although both of us had children of a similar age. It wasn't until my father's funeral when we were forced to communicate that we realized the harm he had caused us. Our children are now the best of friends, as am I with my sister. I can't believe we wasted those ten years.

Writing recriminatory letters or emails never achieves good results. It is so easy to vent your feelings when you are not able to see someone's reactions. However difficult and painful it can be, a face-to-face meeting to try to resolve hurts will be much more effective than writing back and forth.

> When my mother and I fell out over my father's funeral arrangements (he had been married before and I had a very good relationship with my step-brothers) she wanted to explore the disagreement through an email correspondence. She has a very logical way of looking at things and my way is much more emotional. I knew that this method wouldn't work for me so I sent her an email saying that I would not respond to any emails on this subject, and if she really wanted to sort it out we would have to meet face-to-face. When she realized how serious I was about this she agreed to a meeting on neutral territory. It was very painful for both of us when we were forced to see each other's point of view, but we both left the café with a much better understanding and after another meeting we were able to get back on to a much warmer footing.

If you don't feel you can adopt a disinterested approach then at least try not to make things worse. Withdraw yourself from the situation without further acrimony. If you feel it worth it you might follow up with a note to say that you are sorry your attempt was rebuffed but you would still like to make up. After that you may feel that you have done all you can. As mentioned previously, time is a great healer and it is possible that after ruminating for a while the person you approached will come round to your way of thinking. If so, the only thing to remember is not to meet their approaches with a similar rebuff.

The complications of today's extended families seem to cause even more problems of this nature. Should an ex-wife or husband be invited to a funeral, for example? Some might believe not, especially if the divorce was acrimonious. There are other questions that arise:

- What is the position of a long-term partner? More important than a child of the deceased?

- Should step-children rank as importantly as natural children (for example, in seating at the church or in placing in funeral cars)?

- Is a new wife a more important mourner than a parent?

- How do you decide the 'ranking' of children from two different marriages?

Situations like this become even more complicated when there are two or more spouses, more than one ex-partner, a second marriage after the death of a spouse.

My uncle died suddenly. I hadn't been all that close to him but attended his funeral. I noticed that his children, my cousins, made all the arrangements, led the mourning and generally cold-shouldered his second wife (my aunt had died several years before) who was naturally devastated by his death. At the funeral 'wake' she sat alone with just a few friends and they mingled together as a family. I felt dreadfully sorry for her and made an effort to go and speak to her but I could tell that she hardly knew who I was – a niece of his who hadn't even previously met her. I've always remembered that.

If possible, everyone involved should try to remember that the funeral is an occasion of general mourning. Everyone who attends will be upset and anyone's feelings may be easily hurt. If arrangements are complicated it can sometimes help to contact the people likely to feel slighted beforehand.

It is more acceptable to be told 'I was only able to afford two funeral cars and I hope you understand that I felt Roger's children should be in one of them' than to discover that you are relegated to what you may consider a less important place in the funeral procession only when you arrive.

Flattery does help:

'I do hope you can help me out here – you are so good with Auntie Marjorie.'

And so does acceptance of the position:

'You are her son and I would like you to come in the car with me but I'm sure you would prefer to be with your wife and children.'

The will

It isn't only remarks and supposed slights at funerals that cause bad feeling. The contents of a will can cause immense upset and hurt. Even the making of seemingly insignificant bequests can upset family members. Consider remarks like the following:

'I don't see why she thought you would want that picture.'

'I really liked that vase – why has it been especially left to you?'

'My children feel really left out. It's as if their Grandpa didn't love them.'

People often foresee such disagreements and adopt strategies to avoid them happening after their death.

My mother kept an old biscuit barrel on her sideboard. Whenever one of us jokingly referred to wanting to inherit an ornament or some such, she used to say: 'Write it down with the date and put it in the biscuit barrel. If no one else has claimed it I'll write that into my will.' She didn't actually do that but after she died we went through the scraps of paper and it actually helped us to sort out her possessions. There was none of that 'Oh no, I don't want anything really' followed by quiet resentment.

My father began giving away a lot of his books and some of his collections during his final years. It upset us because he didn't ask whether any of us, his children, would like them but gave them away to sometimes virtual strangers. I think now that he was trying simply to avoid any trouble between us after his death.

Sometimes, of course, mutterings about small legacies disguise real resentment about the major bequests in the will. Today's extended and sometimes quite complicated families make any decision about leaving a legacy seem fraught with problems. How, for example, should one provide for the children of a second or third marriage? Should an ex-husband inherit anything? Should all children be treated equally in the will when one or some of them have been more generous with their time and care during their parent's lifetime?

My sister is married to a widower. He has told her that he has left all his estate to his children by his first marriage. We can understand that he would want to provide for them but we worry about what will happen to my sister as she may be left homeless and with only her small pensions to live on.

People often believe that inheritance is their right. You occasionally see letters in magazines where people write in very worried because their mother or father is 'wasting' all their money and children can see 'their' inheritance disappearing. It should be remembered that no one has a right to another's money – not even that of a parent who has died. Everyone is free to spend their money as they wish or to leave it to whom they wish upon their death. The law makes an exception for cases where someone has been a dependent and it does allow certain people to make a claim on the estate if they wish to do so. The Inheritance (Provisions for Dependants) Act in the UK entitles certain people to make a claim on a will. These are:

- surviving spouse or civil partner
- former spouse or civil partner (provided they have not remarried or entered a new civil partnership)
- children (including adult children and anyone whom the deceased treated as their child)
- cohabitees and dependents wholly or partly maintained by the deceased before death.

Although the people named above can make a claim on the estate, the size of any share is not guaranteed and if the relatives who have inherited do not agree with the claim then court proceedings will follow. Not everyone wishes to go down that route.

How else do you deal with what seems an unfair will? There is nothing to prevent those who inherit from giving away their inheritance in order to spread the legacy more fairly. This doesn't seem to happen very often, though. If it is you who has been left out of a will it might seem very difficult to accept. Sometimes a really frank discussion with other family members can resolve matters. You might realize that the money was left to someone who needed it more than you did. You might understand the reasoning behind the bequest and thus find it more acceptable. Often, however, people refuse to discuss money matters and this again can lead to a build-up of resentment which constantly festers and spoils future relationships.

> My mother was estranged from my sister, and I was the only beneficiary of her will. I felt this was very unfair as the fault was very much my mother's and she had done little to engender good relations with either of her children. I decided to split the inheritance 50/50 and divided my sister's half between her two children and it was held in trust until they reached 21. I have no doubt this was the right thing to do.

It can be helpful sometimes if, when writing their will, people explain an unusual bequest or division of their estate. If such an explanation is written in a recriminatory manner, though, this will only make resentment worse. Sometimes it seems that people have a bizarre desire to 'show what they feel' in their will. Suppose such people had come into the open and explained their feelings before death? Consider what a difference this might have made to everyone's relationships.

If, on the other hand, you feel that any bad feeling aroused through the giving of legacies was completely unintentional it might be worth reflecting on how the person who has died might feel if they could see the unpleasantness which has been inadvertently caused. Many people are upset after the death of a parent, a sibling or a spouse, not so much by the tragic occasion but by the behaviour of those left behind. You often hear wise emotions expressed on these occasions:

'I'm going to make sure I write a will.'

'I'll write out a funeral plan so that people don't argue about the funeral service after my death.'

'I couldn't bear to think of my children falling out after I die. I'll make sure I write out my wishes clearly so they understand.'

My grandfather stated clearly in his will that he felt it was for parents to provide for their children and that this was the reason he had not left any individual bequests to his grandchildren. We all understood his reasoning even if we had perhaps hoped for a legacy.

My aunt used her will to vent all her feelings about what she felt was her daughter's lack of care for her. It was all part of a long-standing mother/daughter bad relationship and made us all very uncomfortable. Those who did inherit felt bad and of course her daughter was devastated and has refused to speak to those who inherited until this day. What made it worse was that two of her brothers (who did inherit) tried to offer her what they considered her share and she refused to accept it from them, feeling upset that her mother had reached out to hurt her (as she put it) 'from beyond the grave'.

Unfortunately, good intentions do not always generate wise actions. However, it might be an opportunity for something good to come out of even an acrimonious family funeral if someone makes the effort to reconcile with someone else, if just one person makes sure to write (and sign, witness and date) a will, or if a family at odds with each other decide to get together and act in unison.

Do any of us want to be remembered for the arguments which occurred as a result of our death? Does anyone want bad feelings to be their legacy?

Chapter 6

Personal Effects

After my husband died I started to deal with his personal effects. It kept hitting me like a blow – how easily a person could be apparently 'wiped out'. In a few days documents were cancelled (passport/driving licence), library membership cards were handed in, bank accounts closed, and even clothes disposed of. It began to seem as though he had never existed. I found this eliminating of all the evidence of existence almost worse than the death itself.

Disposing of personal effects

Personal effects are the tangible evidence of someone's existence. Disposing of personal effects after someone has died can be both complicated and harrowing. Wanting to be helpful, friends and relatives often offer to help sort out clothes or take away items which they feel might be giving continual upset to the person who is bereaved. If you have recently been bereaved it might be better if you can resist the urge (and it is a common one) to dispose of things quickly and to allow others to sort things out and take decisions about what should be kept and what disposed of. You may find that a few months down the road you bitterly regret allowing others to make decisions like this.

The urge to sort out and dispose of possessions may seem a little strange but it does seem to be a natural part of the grieving process. It may be that each time something is cleared away or tidied up the mind is able to accept a little more the finality of death. It may be that handling the possessions of a deceased person brings some comfort. If the relationship with the deceased was a difficult one it may be cathartic to clear their things from sight. It may simply be that clearing things out helps the common compulsion to keep busy and avoid thinking too much about sad events.

Some things are easier to dispose of than others. It isn't always the obvious things which we may find difficult to clear out. After a death you may find yourself sweeping through the wardrobes, clearing out books and hobby materials, and selling the car but then finding yourself brought up short by the sight of perhaps a razor on the bathroom shelf, or a lipstick lying forgotten in a drawer.

Aids and applicances

It seems ridiculous but I couldn't bring myself to even open the bag of her possessions which the hospital handed to me after my mother died. I cleared out her clothes and even went through her flat sorting out furniture and other possessions but I couldn't open that bag. In the end my friend suggested that I pop it into a cupboard and go through it later. It was over a year before I was able to do that. I still don't really know why, but I suppose it was something to do with the bag containing the last things she had touched whilst alive.

Often relatives dispose quickly of items which they have come to associate with disablement or unpleasant aspects of the final days of life. Countless wheelchairs, walking frames and walking sticks are deliberately left behind in hospitals or 'donated' to care homes after death. The sad fact is that often these items (which may be both useful and expensive) are quietly binned by the hospital or care home. Raised toilet seats and commodes are not items which people want to either keep or pass on and disposal of them may cause many headaches.

Wheelchairs and walking frames (and indeed walking sticks) are often designed specifically for one person, which means that it is difficult to give them away. For example, the wheelchair used by someone who had multiple sclerosis may be of a different design from one meant for someone who has only minor mobility problems. There are charities who welcome the gift of wheelchairs, but even these may be quite choosey about what type of wheelchair they want to accept. The website http://disabledgear.com lists some of the organizations both in the UK and abroad who welcome donations. Other contacts are listed in the Resources section of this book.

Financial paperwork
Paperwork relating to finances may be one of the first things we deal with simply because it is necessary to get these into order to get probate. However overwhelming the pile may seem to be, it is wise not to throw any papers away without combing through them for important documents. If financial papers are not already filed in some easily accessible way then a good way to start on what seems a monumental and stressful task might be initially to use a loose filing system with piles that can be sorted into:

- anything to do with tax and supporting documents (such as payslips, annual income statements from employers and so on)

- anything to do with property
- any legal documents such as wills, powers of attorney, birth and marriage certificates
- bank statements
- bills, insurance certificates, credit and debit card statements
- anything else financial but not immediately classifiable.

Once you have done this it is easier to sort through papers. After probate has been granted you can deal with papers over a period of time, disposing of all the unnecessary and out-of-date paperwork. Remember that there is a thriving trade in identity fraud and use a secure method such as shredding or burning papers which might be used in this way.

You can find useful information about obtaining probate and dealing with financial details on the UK government website: www.gov.uk//wills-probate-inheritance, see the Resources section for other countries' websites.

After a death there is often a real wish to make sure that in disposing of possessions they are passed on where possible in a way that helps others. This possibly results from a desire to bring meaning to the death, or simply from a wish to do good for others. Some aids and appliances can be recycled quite easily. For example, spectacles are often in demand in the developing world and many optometrist practices and pharmacies have bins where you can simply place no longer required spectacles to be passed on to where they are most needed.

Clothing and personal items

After aids and appliances, the items that often seem most traumatic to sort through and dispose of are items of clothing. This can be particularly harrowing for parents who are mourning the loss of a child. Many of us keep some small items of clothing connected with childhood – a baby's first shoe, a christening robe or an old school uniform cap, for example – after our child (still living) has grown to adulthood. Often we cannot bring ourselves to throw these items away. How much more difficult it is for someone whose child has died before becoming an adult. Perhaps in circumstances like these it sometimes is easier to allow someone else to do the sorting and disposal, or to carry out this task with someone else helping. Remember that everything doesn't have to be done at once. Perhaps it might be easier to start with one class of clothing – say footwear – and then leave the rest until another day.

Disposing of underwear doesn't seem to be a difficult task for most people and yet these items of clothing are the most intimate. Most people throw underwear away unless there are new unworn items which can be passed on.

For some people the grieving can be helped by finding someone to whom items of clothing can be passed on. Many of us have a dislike of throwing away good clothes and it can be a great help to feel that you are doing good or helping others by giving them garments which are in good condition. It can ease the pain of grieving just a little to feel that in death the person you loved is helping others.

> When my husband died there were four brand new shirts in his wardrobe which had never been worn. I really didn't want to bin them nor did I just want to give them to a charity shop. In the office where I worked there was a young ex-student who was just starting his first office job and I heard him one day saying how hard it was to find shirts to fit his large frame. I offered him these new shirts and it was a real pleasure to feel that I had been able to pass them on to someone who appreciated them.

Charity shops are usually only too glad to receive good clothing and there are many around. If the person has died from some particular disease it can help to feel that you are doing good by passing clothing and other effects on to a shop run by a charity which might help others with the same illness such as, for example, in the UK, The British Heart Foundation or Macmillan Cancer Relief. Local hospices also often run charity outlets and might welcome your donations.

It is important to remember that clothing doesn't have to be disposed of all at once. There is no harm in leaving a wardrobe of clothes until one feels able to clear it. Many find it much easier to dispose of one or two items only at a time. It can be tremendously harrowing to handle garments which retain the scent of a loved one and which carry memories in their very fibres. Remember that adult children may like to inherit a garment from a parent. We tend to offer only items such as watches or jewellery as keepsakes, but a piece of clothing which is familiar can be a very acceptable gift.

Service uniform items can be in high demand. Some things like sword belts are very expensive and can be sold through regimental associations and so forth. Other items may be welcomed by local amateur dramatic societies or theatre groups. Particular keepsakes may be welcomed by service museums if they have an association with a regiment or service which is now defunct or if they have associations with a particular conflict. Most newly bereaved people want to keep service medals and in some countries widows/widowers are entitled to wear them on certain occasions. There is, however, a ready market for certain medals.

Some people find the clothing of the deceased very disturbing and want wardrobes and clothes chests cleared quickly – it is quite acceptable to ask another family member or friend to do this for you but, as stated at the beginning of the chapter, this needs to be a decision arrived at without undue pressure from others. Many relatives and friends are glad to feel they can do something specific. If you are a friend of the family and are asked to help sort possessions, consider the request a compliment and give all the help you can even if you find this a difficult task. It is much more difficult for those nearest relatives who are struggling both to come to terms with the shock of bereavement and the huge number of administrative tasks which fall to them in the early days after death. One thing to remember is that clothing is considered to be part of the 'estate' of someone who has died and the value needs to be taken into account when acting as executor of a will.

> My son came to see me during the first few days after my wife died. His second wife came with him. I didn't know her very well but I had no reason to dislike her. She seemed to make my son happy and that was important. However, she was so tactless that by the end of the visit I was near to hating her. She asked me whether she could take away some of my wife's make-up and perfume. I was astounded that anyone could ask for something so personal – especially someone who was not a member of the immediate family – although perhaps she felt that she was!

Sometimes it is considered a nice touch to ask near relatives and friends if they would like an item such as an ornament or a piece of jewellery as a keepsake to remember the deceased. This may actually cause many difficulties. Firstly, the value of any item needs to be noted if probate is to be applied for. Secondly, giving people the chance to choose an item as a keepsake is fraught with difficulties for them. They may fear to choose the item they would really like in case it is too valuable or in case it has happy memories for the bereaved relatives. Many people refuse such offers simply because they are in shock and the very act of taking something which still 'belongs' to the deceased seems like a desecration. Later they may regret their refusal.

One wise idea is to put aside a few items which you would be prepared to give away and offer this limited choice to those you would like to receive a keepsake once the funeral is over and everyone has had time to allow the shock to fade a little. If you are a friend or more distant relative beware of asking for any personal possession of the deceased (even if you feel they wanted you to have it) in the early days.

Disposing of major items

People often contemplate moving house after someone has died. Sometimes this is because a house now seems too big for a widow, widower or surviving partner living alone. Even if this is the case, it is unwise to move house soon after death unless this is absolutely necessary, perhaps for financial reasons or sometimes because the property is a 'tied' house which went with the job of the deceased. In these cases it is usually possible to come to some arrangement with the landlord. Service families are always given a reasonable time before being forced to move out of 'quarters' although they may have to pay a higher rent meanwhile. Houses seem to carry the 'imprint' of the person who has died and they may be full of memories. It is really difficult to come to terms with a death whilst having to deal with the huge upheaval and stress of moving house. If at all possible, it is better to leave any suggestion or contemplation of moving house for at least a year after the death.

Sometimes such a time lag is not possible. For example, it is often true that elderly couples supported each other physically or mentally in ways which an outsider might not have noticed. The death of a partner can make it suddenly obvious that the surviving partner can no longer live alone. This can create a real quandary for relatives or friends trying to help the surviving partner. It is kind to try to keep living conditions as much as possible the same for a few weeks, even if this means that a family member has to move into the house for a short time. It is also important to consult the surviving partner about the future and not, as so often happens, have decisions made by family members because 'of course Mum can't possibly live alone' or 'Dad couldn't manage by himself'. At such times it can help to think 'outside the box'. For example, is there a family member who would accept moving in to the house and helping out in exchange for rent-free/low-rent accommodation? Or perhaps Mum or Dad could go on living in their much-loved family home if a paid live-in carer were to be employed.

Moving house and selling a family home are major projects. They may need to be undertaken after death, but you should try not to rush into such major lifestyle changes if it can possibly be avoided.

My mother was frail and unused to coping alone. We are a large family and for the first few months after Dad died we took turns at staying with her or (sometimes) having her stay with us for a 'holiday'. Meanwhile we talked with her and with each other about the best way forward. None of us wanted to go down the residential care home route but Mum didn't want to live with one of us in case she became a burden. Eventually we found a really nice sheltered housing complex which was relatively near to several of her daughters' homes. It worked out really well, although this option was not cheap. But Mum lived very contentedly there for four years until she died and we felt we had done our best for her.

> The very worst thing about my husband's death was the way the family virtually forced me to take up residence in this care home. I hate it. I know that I probably couldn't have managed alone in our big family house but I could have coped in a small bungalow with some help. I think so, anyway. My family do come to visit but I feel as if I am just a nuisance to them now. It is very hard.

The other major item which commonly has to be disposed of after a death is the car, either because the surviving partner does not drive or because the money from the sale of this item is badly needed. A car often fetches a much smaller price on the open market than is expected and it can be worth thinking about a private sale within the family, perhaps to a young driver who (in exchange) might take on some 'taxi' duties as required. However, it is also worth remembering that there are associated costs to car ownership (tax, insurance, breakdown cover, servicing, for example) and so the actual price fetched from the sale of the car may be intrinsically higher than at first perceived.

Books, hobbies and collections

Many of us have built up collections of things we are interested in, or have items of equipment connected to a hobby we enjoy, or perhaps have a collection of books which we have personally built up over a period of time. It is quite probable that we have never considered what would become of these things in the event of our death. Of course, if a collection is valuable it will need to be valued and itemized as part of the estate of the bereaved, but for many a collection of items or a library of books are of value only for what they have meant to us as individuals with our particular interests. It can be very hard to even consider going through a collection which belonged to someone who has died. The collection evokes the deceased at a very deep level since it is so personal to them. Even if those left behind had no interest in (or perhaps even disapproved of) the hobby or collection involved, it may still be very difficult to consider breaking up the collection, perhaps selling or giving away the equipment or finding some other use for it.

> My husband and I both loved books and we had built up an extensive library. After he died I did not at first consider disposing of any of the books as to me they simply constituted 'our' library. It was only after several months when I was tidying and dusting a shelf that I realized that there were a large number of books in which I had no interest and which I would certainly never read or even open. I could never contemplate throwing them away as to me books are valuable, but I realized that some books were taking up shelf space which could now be put to better use. I had once worked in the book trade and I remembered hearing about Book Aid and this set me on to finding places which could use the books. Those for which no home could be found were given to the local charity shop 'book bank' and I am happy to say that I did not have to throw away a single book.

Hobbies such as fishing or golf often involve the accumulation of quite a lot of expensive equipment. You might consider it a blessing that you are able to donate items like this to someone you know who would value them. Alternatively it is worth contacting the club or association to which the person belonged to see if the club knows of a deserving recipient. A club may also manage the sale of equipment for you and the value of such a sale may be significant. Similarly, collections such as, for example, model railway sets may be valuable and a local club or association would be able to help with the sale or donation of such items. Giving away or even selling a beloved collection can be hard but often the discovery of a fellow enthusiast who can benefit from receiving (or buying) the items can be consoling.

If you are unable to contemplate the handling of equipment, or of previously cherished items, this is a time and a situation where the help of a good friend or an ex-colleague of the deceased can be of great benefit. Do not forget that most people want to help and to be of genuine use after a death. Many would welcome being asked to undertake the task of disposing of sports or hobby equipment, particularly if given a free hand in finding a recipient who would benefit from the gift. If you are asked to undertake such a task by the relative of someone who has died you might consider it a great privilege to be so entrusted. Even if you find the prospect daunting or possibly irritating, it is worth considering how much more daunting it is for the one left behind to have to undertake the task. It might be the last and best service you can do for the deceased.

My friend's wife asked me to sell or give away his collection of guitars after he died. It was difficult for me as I knew very little about the value of the collection and I spent a long time worrying about whether I was giving the right item to the right person and whether I was doing what my friend would have wanted. It actually caused me a couple of sleepless nights! However, another friend happened to say how fortunate I was that I was trusted to do this task and that made me see things in a different light. In the end I stopped agonizing about what my dead friend would have wanted because I reasoned that he would not have wanted me to be so worried about such a thing. It took me quite some time to dispose of all 12 guitars to what I considered 'good' homes but I can honestly say it was a source of great satisfaction in the end and I really felt that I had done a tangible service for my dead friend as well as for his wife.

Some educational and academic books can be used by Book Harvest, an organization which supports Book Aid (see Resources). U3A (The University of the Third Age) groups also are often grateful for donations of educational and text books. The local U3A can be found through the public library or the internet. Scientific and other text books may fetch a high price when sold via universities as they are an expensive outlay for all students. Children's books in good condition may be welcomed by local school libraries or pre-school groups and other books by hospital libraries and second-hand bookshops. Many people find that a selling account at Amazon is a good way to dispose of books. If you have books which do not seem worth selling it is worth donating them to a local charity shop so that others can enjoy them. In some areas there is a 'book bank' run by a charity alongside the recycling bins in local car parks or amenity centres.

One good way to dispose of unwanted items is to use internet sites such as Freecycle. This is a worldwide network of people who believe in the value of giving and getting things free. Freecycle is formed of local groups that match people who have things they want to get rid of with people who can use them. Everything posted must be free, legal and appropriate for all ages. More information is available on their website. Snaffleup is a similar service to Freecycle but it is only UK-based. Gumtree is another website where it is free to advertise any of the goods you would like to dispose of; further, on this website you have the possibility to charge for your goods if you want to. You can also use eBay to sell items which you wish to dispose of.

> My husband was a collector of everything! Our four-bedroom house, loft and large garage were full of his various collections that ranged from stamps and books to ancient suitcases and stationery. After his death my daughter came over and dealt with his clothes, keeping a few bits for the various members of the family and disposing of the rest through the local charity shops and taking what was too far worn to the recycling centre.
>
> Then she got onto the internet to find out about house clearance. In the end the local hospice emptied the loft, which had an enormous accumulation of ancient suitcases, the remains of his office equipment, his out-of-date stationery, etc. Don't forget we have been in this house for over 50 years so there was a lot of stuff dumped up there. Meanwhile we disposed of all the newspaper cuttings he had collected. We just threw them away as no one would be interested in the same subjects as he was. We hope to get rid of his draughting architect's table (I don't know what it is called) by putting it on eBay and the same with other items such as filing cabinets. Slides of subjects he was interested in and his stamp collection are being shown to experts. Someone came along and gave us some money for his books – I also found him on the internet.

The biggest difficulty and heartache may actually arise when it comes to disposing of things which have little or no tangible or even sentimental value. It is possible to feel intensely disloyal when considering throwing away a few CDs, an old pair of boots, a worn wallet or a favourite but chipped mug. As has already been suggested, it may help to ask someone else to 'do the deed' but many of us baulk at something so personal being thrown away even though that is the logical action. Consider whether it may help to retain the item tucked away in a drawer or cupboard out of sight. After many months (or years) it may be easier to dispose of. Or might you adopt the mug or the wallet for your own use? Or keep the old boots by the back door 'in case of visitors'. These kinds of decisions and actions can make life easier in the first months after a death and such items can in this way cease to bring heartache but bring an obscure kind of comfort instead.

Chapter 7

Memorials

It is very natural and normal after a death to feel that you want some kind of memorial. This can be a mixture of the desire to do something constructive to remember the person who has died and also to turn thoughts in a more positive and productive direction. One of our natural fears is that we, or whoever has died, will be forgotten. A memorial is our attempt to prevent that from happening. Perhaps also there is a desire to say: 'This person died but we are still remembering him, therefore in some ways he is still here with us.' Sometimes, whilst still living, people will consider the type of memorial they would like after they die, believing that by doing so they will still be remembered and that their life and death will have meaning.

Perhaps the first step in choosing a memorial is to decide what it is you want to achieve. However, memorials are seldom chosen with such calculated consideration. Sometimes for those who are left behind the memorial becomes a symbol of the life achievements of the deceased. Sometimes the raising of a tangible memorial such as a gravestone becomes a mark of the level of esteem in which the deceased was held by their relatives and friends. Sometimes the memorial may be as simple as an inscription in a crematorium Book of Remembrance. More often the feeling is that a gravestone, a memorial plaque or an urn containing the ashes is the 'proper' type of memorial.

Memorials as a focus of remembrance

In some cases friends and relatives want to ensure that some good comes out of the death of someone they loved. Still others feel that it is important to ensure that any memorial becomes a place where the person who has died can be remembered and their life reflected upon. Often relatives feel strongly that they need a focal point as a place to gather on suitable occasions and anniversaries and a gravestone or a memorial plaque in a Garden of Remembrance fulfils this need.

For some people the ashes of the deceased are a symbol in themselves and where they are placed or how they are disposed of becomes an element of major importance. In some crematoria the ashes can be buried in an urn with a memorial stone.

There are those who wish to carry around a memorial which will always remain a symbol of the essence of the person who has died.

The funeral itself can assume the status of a memorial.

Memorials, then, can take many forms. Everyone has a different idea of what makes a suitable memorial and what seems tasteless to one person becomes a major symbol of the love felt for the deceased by another.

Sometimes people anticipating their death write down their own ideas for their funeral. This can be very helpful for those bereaved who otherwise might spend hours agonizing over details of the funeral service and may later feel that they were rushed or persuaded into some form of service which they later regret. Although it is a comfort at this time for the bereaved relatives to consider what the deceased would have wanted, in the absence of any expressed wishes they may spend time worrying about this or feeling guilty if they are unsure of what those wishes might have been.

No one should feel under any obligation to take everyone's ideas into account (for example, if a relative insists on a particular reading or hymn as being particularly appropriate) although in practice people frequently do. The days immediately after death are a stressful time for everyone concerned and a period of calm and reflection will be beneficial. The funeral is part of the mourning ritual for those who are left behind. It is probably also worth remembering that you are unlikely to be able to please everybody.

Even if no religious funeral service is planned, most people like to have some kind of remembrance service to accompany the burial or cremation. Some people like to call it a 'Celebration of the life of _____' or something similar. Sometimes a member of the family or a close friend of the deceased may lead the ceremony. A non-religious service might take the form of favourite songs and music, poems or other readings and individual remembrances (sometimes called eulogies) by different friends and family. You could display photographs or pictures and other memoranda at the same time.

If you decide to have a memorial stone, make sure you select a memorial mason who specializes in what you are after. In the UK, choose one who belongs to the National Association of Memorial Masons (NAMM) or the British Register of Accredited Memorial Masons (BRAMM) (see Resources for other countries). It is also worth considering whether you should choose a small, independent firm or part of a larger company.

It is worth perhaps taking time to consider the wisdom of paying what can be quite considerable amounts at a time when emotions are running high. The wise option might be to chose the type of memorial that you would like, get all the relevant information and then wait a few weeks or months before making the final decision. Perhaps after some time has passed the need to have an expensive memorial may not seem so important or you might feel that some other thing would be more appropriate. Making major decisions, both financial and emotional, after a significant loss is best delayed for 12 months whenever possible.

Memorial services are sometimes held weeks or months after the actual funeral and these may even take the place of a formal funeral in cases where the body is irreclaimable (such as a death during wartime or an accident which prevents the body being recovered). In many ways a memorial service is similar to a funeral service with readings, songs or eulogies but because a memorial service may be held some time after the death it is often planned more calmly and with more consideration than can be given to a funeral service. A memorial service need not be held in a church or religious building. It could be held in any public place, perhaps even in the open air, and often it may be held in a place which was loved and frequented by the deceased. You might, for example, hold the memorial service on a mountainside if this seems appropriate, or on a boat on a lake, river or sea.

Disposal of the ashes

For some people, the formal 'scattering of the ashes' is a type of memorial service. It is often a chance to invite friends, relatives and acquaintances who were unable to attend the funeral. Because the ashes can be scattered months or even years after the death the whole occasion might have a different atmosphere to a funeral. People might be cheerful and happy and better able to remember the person who has died in a positive way than in the atmosphere of shock and grief of the days immediately after death. Often arrangements for scattering the ashes can be very creative, taking into account the hobbies and interests of the deceased.

There are many ways to dispose of the cremated ashes. These days you can have them blown into space, dispersed in spectacular memorial firework displays or buried in a reef in the sea.

My cousin loved horse racing and after his death we got permission to scatter his ashes actually on the race course. We had to do this before the racing started of course but the occasion was a very happy one. Many friends and relatives came along and we felt that the atmosphere of 'a day at the races' was exactly what he would have liked.

My father often talked about his childhood holidays spent on a farm in the West Country. After he died my sister became quite engrossed with the idea of scattering his ashes on that farm. It was quite complicated to arrange as the farm was no longer a small mixed farm but part of a much bigger concern owned by a big corporation. However, the effort that she put into getting permission, organizing the occasion and finally carrying out the actual scattering was clearly somehow cathartic to her and this became her personal memorial to him.

To many it is important that any memorial to the deceased is not only tangible but fitting as a way to remember them. Many like the idea of a bench placed in a situation often frequented by the person who has died. This is one reason why we often encounter benches inscribed with loving memorial words in quite unusual places.

If you are planning to place a bench in someone's memory you will have to ensure that you obtain permission to do so. Some popular places are becoming so full of strategic benches that restrictions are placed on where they are sited.

> When my mother died she specified that she wanted her ashes to be scattered at sea. She loved the sea with a passion and always went to a particular beach so it felt entirely right that she should be a part of it although we would have preferred her to have been buried so that we would have to place to visit. Her grand-daughter suggested that we ask for a bench to be placed on the beach facing the sea where we scattered her ashes so that we could come and sit and remember her. The council agreed and I know she would have approved.

Another very popular form of memorial is to plant a tree, a shrub or a bush.

> My husband loved lemons and so we planted a lemon tree in our back garden. Every year it produces lemons! I always felt that was a very appropriate memorial to him: simple, natural and very apt.

You might plant a tree in a wood. Trees have a long life and it can be very moving when out for a walk to come upon a tree with a plaque beside it giving details of the person for whom it is a living memorial. There are organizations such as Life for a Life which specialize in setting up memorial forests where, if desired, the cremated ashes can be buried next to the memorial tree you have chosen to plant. If you wish to plant a tree in an existing wood you will of course need permission from the owners, but there is nothing to prevent you planting a tree in your own garden or grounds.

Bushes and shrubs are popular and long-lasting memorials and if you desire you can keep the shrub in a large pot so that if you move house it can go with you. You can even combine a memorial plant with disposal of ashes by burying the ashes in the plant pot. There are a huge number of plants and many people like the idea of buying a plant with the same name as the deceased. In the UK, the Royal Horticultural Society website (see Resources for other countries) can be helpful for finding a plant with the right name but many garden centres also have systems to help you with this. If you cannot find a plant with the right name you might prefer to choose a plant which flowers around the time of the deceased's birthday or some other date that is special.

> When my father-in-law died I bought a clematis which had his name and placed it in a large pot with a brass label on my mother-in-law's patio. She drew great comfort from looking after it and later from just sitting out near the plant, quietly contemplating the past.

> My 'memorial flower bed' started with the death of my grandmother when I dug up a small shrub from her garden and moved it to mine in her memory. Then when my elderly aunt died I bought a rose which had her name. Later I carried on adding plants in memory of my mother, my father, two cousins and an old friend. The garden gives me a tangible memorial and many hours of pleasure.

There are so many different choices for memorials, especially in a time when technology is opening up new possibilities.

A firm called Eternity Crystal has pioneered and patented the process of fusing a small amount of the ashes from a cremation into crystal glass keepsakes and they can also make ashes or the hair of the deceased into jewellery. They only require a small quantity of ashes or hair so that multiple memorials can be made for a family, whilst the deceased can still be laid to rest in a chosen place.

It is also possible to make the ashes into a diamond. High-quality diamonds can be created from the carbon as a memorial.

There is a free tribute service run by the MuchLoved Charitable Trust based in the UK and set up in the early 2000s by Jonathan Davies who lost his brother very suddenly at the age of 21. Jonathan wanted to set up an online memorial to his brother and one that would be easy for his brother's friends to view and develop but there was nothing available at the time. However, when technology moved on to the extent that it was easy to upload pictures and videos, MuchLoved was born.

You can have photographs made into professionally published hardback books or arrange for videos, pictures and stories to be collated to form a legacy. These often come with price tags that range from hundreds to thousands of dollars or pounds and a family might consider that they could make their own memorial book/electronic record which would achieve the same result and be a true 'labour of love' on behalf of the deceased.

> My son spent many hours making up, copying and sending to all our relatives an electronic copy of photographs taken throughout my husband's life from the time he was a baby until a few hours before his death. Some relatives appreciated the thought very much and wrote to thank him. Others made no comment. But I truly believe that the effort he put into making this memorial helped him come to terms with his own grief.

Many people want to feel that a memorial is not just a way of remembering but perhaps can be a vessel for doing good for others – perhaps other people who are suffering from the same condition which caused the death of the deceased. Sometimes the memorial might take the form of supporting a cause in which the deceased took a keen interest. Leaving a legacy to charity is an excellent way to make a memorial in a way which will make your generosity last beyond your lifetime. If you decide to make a charity a beneficiary you'll need to know the full name and registered charity number. Funeral directors will usually arrange to have donations given at the funeral sent directly to a nominated charity and it is quite fashionable now to specify 'no flowers – donations to charity' on funeral notices.

Some charities now have a tribute fund facility whereby you can set up a tribute fund in the name of your loved one with all monies collected going to the charity. It gives a focus for you and your family and friends to concentrate your fundraising efforts in the name of the person you are remembering. Usually there is a facility for families and friends to view online the status of the fund and to see how different fundraising efforts (for example, from funeral collections, a sponsored run or a memorial auction) are being collated in the name of the person who has died.

Sometimes those who wish to mark their remembrance in a special way will undertake a sponsored event in the name of the person who has died, afterwards donating the proceeds to a suitable charity. Often walks or sponsored events are used as a fundraiser towards a material memorial, such as much-needed equipment for a hospital or a special garden attached to a care centre. However, you need to be aware that some charities find that donations which are 'ring fenced' for a particular item or for use in only one area of the country can be difficult for them to administer. Indeed, some charities will actually negotiate with you to try to get your agreement for donations to be used where they see the most need and not where you would like the money to go. There are two sides to this. On the one hand it can be very difficult if resources are badly needed in one area and donations are being made which specify their use in another area and the charity concerned may wish that you would trust them to use the money in the best possible manner. On the other hand many people are very concerned at the possibility of large sums of money being spent on funding prestigious 'headquarter buildings' or (even) finding their way into bonus money paid to chief executives and want to be sure that their memorial is used in a fitting manner where it will reach people in need of the services the charity provides. You may wish to discuss with the charity where money is most needed and then consult with other donors if you are taking part in a group effort as a memorial. It may be that everyone concerned will be happy for the money to be used where the charity indicates it is needed. In any case, most charities must accept that donations are 'donor led' if you insist on money donated being used for a particular purpose.

My husband had dementia and many of his happiest hours in his last months of life were spent in the local Alzheimer's Society day centre where the staff also gave the whole of our family a great deal of support. I wanted to buy something for the day centre and in the end I gave the money for a 'Sensory garden' to be made in the grounds. I go there myself now and again to visit and always get great consolation from seeing others enjoy his memorial.

Care and residential homes

Memorials in care and residential homes are valuable because they can unite the care workers, families and residents and allow them to grieve together. There are many ways to arrange this. For example, a table can be set up in the lounge with a photo of the person who died. It can be a photo with a small fresh vase of flowers The photo can be a recent one or one taken some time previously with a short life history attached to it. A small book for people to write their memories in can be placed on the table. Information about the funeral can be pinned to a notice board above the table and information about the funeral tea, which can be held at the home after the funeral, will add an important and inexpensive touch.

A one-minute silence in the dining room can take place either on the day of the death or on the day of the funeral. The residents will know that when their time comes there will be a one-minute silence for them, too, and they will be remembered.

It is possible to respect and celebrate someone's life simply by talking about them and remembering them and a memorial can be central in including the home in a positive way.

Another idea is to set one afternoon in the year aside as a day for remembering everyone who has died. A tea can be held in the care home, and the families of those who have died during the year can be asked if they would like to bring either sandwiches, biscuits or a cake. The care workers can attend and meet up with the families and everyone can remember their family member who passed away during the year. It will be an opportunity for the care workers to meet up again with family members who they possibly became quite close to, for the family members to talk to the care workers about their relative (who perhaps knew them better than anyone else at the end of life), and for the other residents to realize that they too will be remembered. Similarly, it would be nice to plant a tree, or a bush, in memory of all those who died. Again, this is not a big expense in financial terms but the rewards will be felt throughout the home. Dignity and respect will have found a place to reside and that ethos can only benefit all involved.

Some homes have a memorial garden or some other way of recognizing the part that individuals have played in the life of the home. Often it is very helpful for those left behind to do something to recognize the part played by the carers in a residential home. Donating a garden bench, or an item of equipment, or planting a special flower bed in the garden are all ways of doing this. The manager of the home will often be very supportive in helping relatives to decide what gesture to make.

Because the emotions are still engaged long after the memories have begun to be lost, people with dementia may like to be included in memorial occasions such as visiting a grave, drinking a toast on the birthday of the person who has died, looking at photographs or watching DVD footage. However, they may forget that the person is dead and become confused, looking around for them or asking where they are. This does not mean that you should exclude them from these occasions but it is as well to decide on an individual basis whether they will find it more upsetting than reassuring.

Signs of mourning

There is a tradition in many cultures for the wearing of a specific colour as a sign of mourning. The colour chosen is often, but not always, black (white is considered appropriate in many cultures). This tradition was common in western society in the past two centuries with the mourner wearing dark or black clothes for some time after a death. In Victorian times this was taken to considerable excess and a widow would wear deepest black and not leave the house for several weeks. She would only appear in public heavily veiled and might wear a particular form of headdress – the 'widow's cap'. Men, too, wore unrelieved black. Mourning was only gradually 'lightened' over a period of months so that one might slowly begin to wear grey or very sober colours. The final stage in this mourning was the wearing of black gloves for women and a black tie or black mourning armband worn on the left arm between the shoulder and elbow for men. The black armband has traditionally been recognized as a symbol of mourning and was a signal to the community that the wearer was bereaved.

Unfortunately, along with many other mourning traditions, this tradition has fallen into disuse in the western world, although it does still remain in some cultures and on some public occasions, for example, where the wearer of a black armband wishes to identify with the commemoration of a comrade or team member who has died.

As described earlier, the end of the tradition of wearing black or a black armband has meant that those in mourning no longer have an external sign of their internal emotional state, and for this reason we strongly advocate the wearing of an external symbol – a purple leaf – to allow the mourner to make known that they have suffered a loss. The leaf symbol can be worn as a brooch, a lapel pin or a necklace. It can be worn for as long or short a time as required and is a fitting memorial which can be brought out in the future and worn on days when the mourner is feeling particularly sensitive, no matter how long has passed since the death occurred. Families may find solace in wearing the leaf or even in distributing leaf brooches to mourners at the funeral (www.endoflifebook.com/leaf-pin).

If you have an unusual idea for a memorial and you feel that it is a fitting and appropriate way to remember someone who has died then there is no reason why you should not go ahead with putting your idea into practice. However, it is well to remember that there will be many friends and relatives of the deceased who might like to be consulted or at least considered.

Perhaps the best and most lasting memorial to anyone who has died is the difference which their passing makes to the lives of those left behind.

> After my wife died I volunteered to work in the local hospice even though she had not died there. I can honestly say that it is the best decision I ever made. My life has been transformed by my volunteer work and in my heart I think of it as my own memorial to her.

The passing of a loved one causes grief and distress but sometimes good can come out of the event. Survivors often point to the death of a loved one as the catalyst which began a new journey in their life. Perhaps they changed jobs and began working for a charity or support organization. Perhaps they took up a cause and put their energies into achieving good for others. Perhaps they changed their attitude and decided to stop worrying and to 'seize the day' or make other changes to their lifestyle which would help them get the best out of life. Conversely, there are those who find it very difficult to continue with life after the death of a loved one. These people may sink into a depression and spend their days asking, 'What is the point?' It can be thought-provoking to consider the effect that death has on our lives as a memorial to the person who has died. What sort of memorial is our life, post-bereavement?

Chapter 8

Anniversaries

The time after a death is full of anniversaries:

'Yesterday he was still alive.'

'This time last week I was visiting her in hospital.'

'The funeral was exactly a week ago.'

'A month ago today she died.'

'This week would have been his birthday.'

'This will be the first Christmas I have been on my own.'

Anniversaries are hard after bereavement and they can be very personal to us. As well as major events such as the first Christmas, the first birthday of the deceased, and the anniversary of the death itself, there are the small occasions in the life of every relationship which are between those in the relationship. What about the fact that your mother used to buy you a bar of chocolate every Saturday; your father would always remember the day you passed your driving test; you and your husband always watched a favourite TV programme; your daughter always came out shopping with you on the first Friday of the month? These small 'anniversaries' hit very hard at first because there is probably no one with whom to share them. Even close friends or other family members may think that feeling sad over a missing bar of chocolate is taking your grief a step too far. The truth is, of course, that it is not the missing bar of chocolate that counts – it is the fact of your mother thinking of you, the little routine which showed that you were loved and the enormous impossible-to-ignore truth that she is now no longer around. At first some people may try to keep to the routine. Perhaps you buy yourself a bar of chocolate, but then the realization comes that this really doesn't help – it doesn't bring your mother back and, often, it doesn't ease the sense of loss. We all find our way through this maze of the 'little anniversaries' in our own manner. Some people may find a complete change of routine helps. Others substitute another ritual for the one which is lost. These small occasions are poignant and we generally learn to manage them alone because others are often not aware that they even exist.

Christmas

Some times are always more difficult than others. Christmas is a family occasion for many and may be especially difficult for many years after bereavement. Family and friends tend to understand this and invitations around this time are likely to be generally welcome. However, if you are grieving you may dread such invitations whilst welcoming the kind thoughts behind them. You may feel that you will be unable to bear the forced jollity and family atmosphere. You may be uncomfortably aware that for you Christmas can never be the same again. If you are the child of a surviving parent you may wonder how you can fill the empty gap left by the absence of Mum or Dad. If you are a parent who has been widowed you may be overwhelmed at the need to make Christmas a happy time for your grieving children.

During the weeks and days leading up to Christmas, thoughts and memories of the person who died may occupy your mind and cast a shadow over the time leading up to the day. It may be that at this season more than at any other time you feel overcome by grief and despair. Everyone around seems to be in a festive mood and it may seem churlish to cast any gloom over the proceedings.

The surprising thing is that feelings of sadness and gloom are actually very common around Christmas. The suicide rate climbs at this time of the year and there are thousands of people who, if asked to express their real feelings, will tell you that they hate Christmas. There may be many reasons behind these feelings: the darkness of the time of year (in the northern hemisphere at least), the feelings of isolation and loneliness engendered when everyone around you seems to be partying, annoyance at what seems to be a false sense of jollity, despair at the commercialization of a religious feast, perhaps even the knowledge that after the fun and abandon of the feast the same old dreary routine will still be there. If you are dreading Christmas then you are not alone.

> It is six years since my husband died and I still find Christmas a very difficult time. We had made so many small family 'traditions' around the occasion. The first year I had several kind invitations from friends and family and in the years since I have managed always to arrange a way to get through the season – I even still enjoy the anticipation. But always, at some point on the day, I find myself thinking about him and missing the small things he used to do or say. It is hard then because you do not want to speak about these things in front of family and friends who are enjoying themselves.

The knowledge that you are not alone may not help you at this time, though. You will still feel that you need to get through the festival and probably you hope not to upset others or let your grief intrude on their enjoyment.

One idea might be to look ahead and decide for yourself what your Christmas plans are so that, when well-meant invitations come along, you can say 'thanks but no thanks' with sincerity and calmness. You could, for example, go away for Christmas. Many hotel chains have 'Christmas specials' deals which are aimed at those who are alone. Of course you may feel apprehension at going somewhere like this alone but you may be pleasantly surprised at the enjoyment you gain from the time away – and if you do not, well at least you made your own plans and no one need worry about you this year. Next year you can think again.

Or you might invite a friend or friends (or other family members) who are in a like situation to spend Christmas with you. You could plan a joint effort with each person bringing an item of food or a festive contribution ('You bring the crackers, Kate will bring the turkey and I'll supply the drink'). Even if things go wrong or something is forgotten you can laugh about it together.

You may actually prefer to take yourself well away from the action and jollity and if this is your choice no one should deny you – just be sure that it *is* your choice and that you are not choosing this option because you think you will only cast a dampener on others' Christmas cheer. It can help to remember that you are probably not the only person who is grieving. Many a widow or widower has gone along with Christmas plans of their children in order not to upset them without realizing that they too may be feeling the huge gap left this holiday season by the absence of Mum or Dad. If you think this may be the case you might plan a little touch to the celebrations which will help everyone in their time of grieving.

> My father-in-law had a particular toast which he always made at the Christmas dinner. After he died, my husband took over the tradition. When my husband died I asked my son to make the toast at our first Christmas dinner and he told me afterwards, in private, that he felt very keenly the honour at being asked to 'carry on the torch' of family tradition.

In Chapter 4 on More About Grief we strongly recommend the benefits of volunteering. This might be a good time to consider spending your Christmas day or holiday period caring for others in a voluntary capacity. Charities for the homeless, for example, are often looking for volunteers over the Christmas period and there are certain to be other charities who need help around that time of year. Many people have considered volunteering at Christmas but have felt unable to do so because of other family commitments. Perhaps this 'first Christmas' anniversary is the time to reconsider the idea. If looking for volunteering possibilities around the Christmas period do not leave it too late in the year to do so.

If you, as a concerned friend or relative, ask someone who is grieving to a family Christmas meal in the weeks or months after a death it is worth thinking carefully beforehand. It can be hard for anyone to be part of a different family on this day and not know their customs and 'in jokes'. Allow the recently bereaved some quiet time if they seem to want it and don't feel you must 'jolly them along'. A good idea is to ask them to bring along an item of food or organize some part of the proceedings. Maybe this is the year to make a change to your own 'traditional Christmas'.

Mum came to us for her first Christmas after Dad died. All the family used to telephone each other on Christmas morning – the phone was always red hot. I had the idea of putting Mum 'in charge' of the phone. This meant that she got to talk to everyone first; it gave her an important job in the proceedings; and frankly it was a great help to me as I scurried around organizing the meal.

Planning ahead

Whatever that anniversary is, whether it is a birthday, the anniversary of the death, or perhaps a wedding anniversary it is well worth thinking ahead and preparing for the occasion and considering the most beneficial way to spend it. It can be that the anticipation of 'the day' is worse than the day itself. A birthday, whether yours or that of the person who has died, can be a very distressing and lonely occasion. Often friends or family will anticipate this and rally round. Do not automatically refuse an invitation if one is given to spend the day with others. You might feel that you would prefer to spend the day alone but, like all anniversaries, the day has to be got through and friends and family can help. This is where your preparation and thinking ahead can help. If you know that you will be unable to face any planned outing with others then make it known in advance that you have your own plans. However, you could suggest that you do something with your friends and/or family at a later date so that they understand not only that you have thought and planned ahead but that you are not rejecting their well-meant offers of support.

On the other hand you might be glad of some distraction and some way of getting through the day without too much sadness. You could ask a special friend in advance to spend the day with you and have an outing planned. It could be something as simple as a quiet lunch out somewhere or a trip to some place nearby which you have always enjoyed visiting. You might go to see a film or watch a sporting event or simply visit the shops. In this way you can mark the day without too much sorrow or distress.

Some people actually like to plan an event connected with the deceased to take place on an upcoming birthday. A number of people plan to scatter the ashes on a birthday or anniversary in order to mark the occasion; and although some might accuse you of being morbid, many will understand your actions as making a meaningful point of what might otherwise be a very sad time.

First anniversary of death

The first anniversary of death is difficult. You may want to visit the grave or memorial stone, say a prayer in church, light a candle or drink a toast to the one who has died. You may choose to get the family together to do some remembering. If the death was the result of an accident there are those who wish to return to the site to lay flowers and to have a small ceremony of remembrance if appropriate. There are some who do not wish to mark the occasion in any way and see this as a day to be got through and forgotten as expeditiously as possible. However you choose to spend the day, do not let others suggest you are being morbid or depressive or even perhaps disrespectful to the memory of the dead. For this first anniversary of death it is good to plan ahead and to treat yourself gently.

For some, the anniversary of the death may be about reliving the last moments, or if the death was unexpected perhaps thinking about what you could have done differently. It can be a time of regrets and a lot of 'if only's and 'what if's.

There may be others who loved the person who died and perhaps these are the people you are able to spend time with and share your emotions. Like you they will still miss the person you are remembering.

> On the anniversary of my sister's death in an air crash someone suggested that I plan a balloon release. I invited close friends and family. Before they arrived I bought a purple balloon, which was her favourite colour. I cut several oblong pieces of paper in different colours and punched a hole in the corner of each one. When the guests arrived I asked each person to write down a memory they had of my sister. We went to a nearby park, and each person read aloud the memory and threaded the slips of paper onto the balloon string. We then released the balloon, letting it, and the attached memories, drift away.

> Every year I get together with my ex-wife, daughter and some of my son's friends and we have a party to remember and celebrate my son's life. It is very sad but in some way very comforting to be with other people who care.

Perhaps a slightly unusual way to spend the day is with the person who has died. Consider perhaps writing them a letter, lighting a candle, playing the music they loved, talking to them in whatever way feels natural to you. You can speak out loud or internally, and if you just want to get drunk or pour out your emotions in tears – feel free to do that too.

On the anniversary of my daughter's death I always look at photographs. It brings floods of tears which continue until I put the photos away again but somehow with the 'letting go' my body feels relieved and lighter – ready to go on…

One of the theories of grief is continuing bonds – that you continue to have a relationship with the person who died (Klass 1996). It is the basis of many religions and can make a lot of sense.

On the first anniversary I found myself writing a letter to my dead daughter. I managed to write several pages of memories as if she were able to receive this letter. Foolish? Maybe, but it really helped and it made me feel connected again.

If you have had a long-term relationship with someone, then the fact that they are no longer alive doesn't mean that your relationship dies with them. Death brings a life to an end but doesn't end the relationship. You can still have a relationship, however odd that may sound. Talking to the person that died, although it may sound as though it is a reason for spending some quiet time in a padded cell, can be very therapeutic. Continuing to talk to them, to think about what they would have liked or disliked, or noticing something that you know would have amused them, is far healthier than feeling you have to stop any interaction overnight. Learning to live with the fact that someone who has died is no longer with you is hard enough, but having to stop conversing with them is an additional and unnecessary hardship.

Starting your own tradition on the anniversary of the death or on the anniversary of the birthday of the person who died gives it a different focus and is one way of coping with those 'difficult days'.

I dreaded the anniversary of my son's birthday every year after he died. Every anniversary reminded me of how much I had lost. The shadow of that day loomed larger and larger every year and I started to get more and more depressed as the time ticked towards the day. Someone suggested that I start my own tradition on his birthday and this idea saved me. I decided I would invite the family to a weekend in Cornwall and on the anniversary of his birthday we would all go to ·his favourite beach and throw flowers and rose petals into the sea. No matter what the weather, this is what we do every year. Sometimes it is only me and my husband who go – sometimes other members of the family join us. But instead of dreading the approach of the anniversary I am busy organizing the weekend. The grief is still there but somehow the enormous black shadow that hung over the period surrounding that day has diminished.

Moving on

During the initial grieving period the people in your environment will hopefully be aware and sensitive to your emotions, but as time goes on, when anniversaries arrive, few people may understand how difficult those days are for you. It is for this reason that we have designed a small leaf-shaped brooch (see Chapter 4). This brooch was designed as an external symbol of grief to make people aware that you are experiencing a difficult time due to a death and it is also a thoughtful gift to give to those who are grieving. You might like to wear it as just a small acknowledgement of the importance of this day. We have also designed special cards for anniversaries (see our website www.endoflifebook.com for details). The 'Still Remembered' cards are not available in the shops and express a simple message to let others know they are not forgotten in their grief. It can be a great comfort to someone to know that you have remembered them at this time.

Some churches have a special service (usually in November around All Saints or All Souls day) when they read out the names of those who have died that year and perhaps light candles in their memory. Even if you are not a regular churchgoer you may find this comforting and you might like to suggest to a friend or family member who wants to be helpful and kind that you would appreciate their company at this service. Some Jewish people observe *yahrzeit*, and light a yahrzeit candle on the anniversary of the death.

Not all religions observe the first anniversary of death and of course not everyone wants to be involved in any religious observance at this time. But cards of remembrance, lighting candles in someone's memory, looking at photographs of the deceased and getting together to remember and reflect on someone's life are all ways to mark an anniversary and some people will find comfort in these actions.

The days after the first anniversary of a death can be more difficult than we think. There is a tendency on the part of well-meaning friends and relatives to think that once the first anniversary of the death is over everything will be back to 'normal'. If we are grieving we may even have this feeling ourselves.

Actually one of the hardest times for me was the first few weeks after the first anniversary of my mother's death. Unconsciously I suppose I had thought that after this anniversary everything would be different. When after a few weeks I came to the realization that it wasn't – that I still missed her just the same – that she would still not be coming back to me, I became very depressed.

There is the expectation that after the first anniversaries are over the bereaved person is now ready to move on. But in some ways after the first anniversary the bereaved person may find themselves realizing for the first time that this loss is permanent and any expectation that they will be able to move on after the first year is premature. This period may in fact be the time when support is most needed. If you find that the anniversary has been deeply painful and you feel that you need someone to talk to, Befrienders Worldwide (Samaritans in the UK) are available 24 hours a day seven days a week and are not only for those who are contemplating suicide but also for those in emotional pain.

The harsh fact is that anniversaries never stop. After the first Christmas without the deceased there is another one. After the first anniversary of the death there will come the second and subsequent anniversaries. Some people may find that each year these times of remembrance get easier but, as we have seen, for some this is not the case.

If you are supporting someone who is grieving, try to avoid suggesting that the anniversary is the time they should 'move on'. It is less than helpful to make remarks such as:

'He wouldn't have wanted you to grieve this much.'

'Now the anniversary is past it is really time you moved on.'

'You are upsetting your children.'

'Try not to think about it any more.'

None of us is perfect and it is easy to let remarks such as this slip out; but if you can, try to keep to quiet sympathy and let your actions speak for you. Now is the time to send a 'Still Remembered' card, to suggest a future outing to look forward to, to go with someone to the graveside or to a remembrance service, to just be there as a friend.

> After my closest friend lost her husband I planned an outing on the first anniversary of his death which involved going to a local garden they had both loved visiting followed by lunch at a restaurant of her choice. The following year she asked me if we could do this again and now it has become a tradition but it no longer feels sad. Instead we plan what part of the garden we are going to spend most time in and she and I take it in turns to choose the place where we are going to eat lunch. It is always a quiet outing but in a way it has turned into a happy tradition. One year I asked if she wanted to do something different but she said that although she no longer felt sad during the outing it made her feel closer to her husband and she asked if I minded carrying on. He was her husband but they were both friends of mine and of course I miss him too so it is a good day for both of us each year.

We cannot hide from the fact of anniversaries. We can only give some thought to how we want to spend them and to whether we want them to haunt our lives in the future. An anniversary can be a most difficult and testing time but it can also be a time of sweet remembrance. Although there are many anniversaries and the anniversary of a death will return again and again, most people can come to terms with managing these occasions. If you find that this is not the case, if the thought of the death and the anniversaries afterwards are coming to dominate your thinking, then it may be that you would find some professional help useful. In this chapter we have already mentioned that Befrienders Worldwide or the Samaritans will be willing to help if you feel you need to talk to someone who can be objective. There are also many bereavement counselling services and you should not feel that just because the death is some time in the past you are not eligible to access these services. They are available at any time. A list of some bereavement counselling services is included at the back of this book in the Resources.

Chapter 9

Beyond Tomorrow

To paraphrase Scarlett O'Hara in *Gone with the Wind*, tomorrow is another day. Surely an obvious statement, but for someone just bereaved each day can seem an endless stretch of time, and to contemplate tomorrow when one has just woken to the darkness of today is impossible.

Many people hope and long for the day when they will be able to move 'beyond tomorrow' and away from the darkness and depression that seems to engulf them after the death of someone close. Often, especially in the early days following a death, it will seem that such a time can never come. Some people may actually not want to consider that they will ever recover from their grief because recovery seems a kind of disloyalty to the person who has died.

The truth is that in some ways we never come to terms with the death of someone close. That death becomes part of what makes us who we are. In this sense it is always with us and is always a part of us, it shapes us and colours our outlook on the world.

Some people hope that looking beyond tomorrow *will* mean coming to terms with the death and being able to put any negative emotions behind them. Others simply hope that coming to terms with the death may mean feeling that they have an ability to get enjoyment out of life in spite of their loss.

In order to move forward after a death there needs to be a healthy grieving process (see Chapter 4 on More About Grief). Although grief is an ongoing process and we may consider that it never ends, it is still a process that has to happen, and the process should not be prevented in any way from taking its course. Allowing yourself to experience your feelings plays a crucial part in the healing process.

Grieving involves experiencing pain and, of course, pain is unpleasant. Sometimes grief is so all-encompassing that there is a fear of feeling overwhelmed and losing control and so we may look for a short cut – a way to avoid our feelings of grief or believe that if we bury ourselves in work or throw ourselves into family life and support everyone around us we will be able to avoid the worst of it. However, those who don't allow themselves to grieve because they don't want to 'let the side down', or because they are being 'strong' for others, may find themselves totally unprepared for the grief when it does come.

> My ex-husband said that the death of my mother when I was 16 had ruined me. I nursed her and never properly grieved for her and I think it made me stronger but not necessarily in a good way.

Moving on

Successfully moving beyond tomorrow depends a lot on our past experiences and on our feelings about those experiences.

For example, someone who had a close and loving relationship with their partner paradoxically may be more open to meeting others, therefore perhaps achieving some sense of closure by starting another loving relationship. On the other hand, someone whose relationship was acrimonious may feel that they are better off alone and might be less open to another potentially loving partnership. Moving beyond tomorrow by way of forming a new relationship may be more difficult for them as negative memories of their past relationship may be constantly impeding their present.

Moving on is about being adaptable. After someone has died we have to adapt to a life without their presence, perhaps without the support and help they once gave, certainly without their company. Adaptability is often (but not always) related to age. Couples in many long-term relationships often have fallen into a comfortable division of responsibilities which works for them and which allows each to use their strengths and to surrender to the other the life area in which they feel least comfortable. In some relationships the handling of financial matters is left to one person. Frequently, especially in the older generation, the cooking and household tasks are left in the hands of the female partner. Sometimes all the driving is undertaken by one member of the partnership. In relationships where there was a high level of dependency in one area the surviving partner may find their life complicated and made more difficult by the need to assume a role with which they are not familiar and which they find uncomfortable.

A feeling of being disempowered by all the responsibilities that need to be taken on, or the thought of a future full of yet-unrehearsed roles, can prevent a bereaved person from moving forward with confidence. It is a challenge to look beyond tomorrow when there is a whole area of your life that is not mastered or feels unattainable.

As a bereavement counsellor it occurred to me recently that single older men whose mothers had died seem to have enormous difficulty in moving on and find it almost impossible to achieve any kind of closure. Perhaps because their mother in some ways covered different roles, of both being a parent and companion. Also the men's caring for that parent filled their days with meaning.

Sorting out the possessions of the person who has died and giving them a good and loving home, wherever possible, is also a part of achieving a sense of finality (see Chapter 6, Personal Effects). Some people take this task on with an excess of enthusiasm and later regret throwing away some items. Others find it impossible to contemplate and wardrobes and boxes remain full, often for years. At first it is a great sadness to approach the task of 'clearing out' and so this may be put off. Later on there seems no point, and perhaps one gets used to turning away from the stuffed drawers and cupboards. An older person may find the task infinitely tiring. In such a case it may be better to enlist help. Sometimes, however, younger family members may, whilst meaning to help, take thoughtless actions and cause great sorrow.

I remember, after my father died, my two sisters helping my Mum to clear out Dad's things. I was absolutely amazed later to hear that they had burned my father's bed on a huge bonfire. When I asked why, my sister retorted 'Well, would you have wanted to sleep on it?' but I know my mother was devastated and felt as if by this action they were somehow wiping my Dad out of existence.

It is a kind gesture to offer to help clear the belongings of someone who has died but such an action must be done with great sensitivity. What seems like useless rubbish to you may be items bursting with memories to the one left behind. It is a task not to be undertaken lightly. It doesn't really matter if 'clearing out' is left for a while. Some people prefer to do this little by little, perhaps tackling a drawer or a box now and again when they feel up to it.

The clothing of the deceased is always very emotive. The scent can linger on clothes and will be a subconscious but constant reminder. It may be difficult to give clothes away as others don't want to literally wear 'dead man's shoes'. On the other hand it may seem wasteful to throw clothes away. One option is to pass clothes fit for use on to a charity shop thereby feeling that one is doing some good, especially if a favourite charity of the deceased is chosen to benefit.

It is often only after being left a widow or widower that one realizes how much this world is dominated by couples. Food is sold in packs of two, special offers for shows are often based on two tickets, restaurants offer two meals for the price of one, hotel offers are 'based on two people sharing a double room'. Invitations are less forthcoming once one is single, simply because people like to balance the numbers and feel they must always invite guests in pairs. Becoming suddenly a single person in a world that was once inhabited by couples is extremely painful and lonely. It takes an effort to make a new life with other widows or widowers when an effort is the last thing you feel capable of making.

The circumstances of the end of life will also have a major impact on the person's ability to move on. A very sudden and unexpected end of life will have its own complications but need not ultimately prevent a form of closure. The suddenness and expectedness of the loss can make acceptance very difficult. There is a tendency to dwell on the reasons leading up to the death and to constantly refer to 'if only' in one's thoughts.

Conversely, it is often very hard to come to terms with a death which has been protracted and drawn out. First of all there is a loss of role. The days once filled by caring for the person at the end of life now stretch aimlessly ahead. Those left behind may need to go over and over the final days and weeks of life and examine how things might have gone differently. It is no good telling someone to try not to think of it. Frequently it is the very last thing one wants to think of, but the unpleasant scenes keep re-occurring in the thoughts however much one tries to avoid them. Sometimes it is a good form of therapy to talk about what happened. Those who are trying to help someone through grief should try to have patience even if it means listening to the same thoughts and reflections several times. Sometimes the best people to talk with are other family members who will also want to use this discussion as a kind of therapy; but if you would prefer to speak to an empathic stranger, Befrienders Worldwide or the Samaritans are always on the end of the phone.

Holding a funeral or other end-of-life ceremony is key in achieving any sense of finality. Those who are unfortunate enough to experience someone they loved go missing, whether or not it occurs during a war or conflict, often cannot achieve any closure until the person is found either alive or not. Some families after the Falklands conflict only came to terms with the death after their loved ones were exhumed and returned 'home' even though those soldiers had been given a proper burial on the Falkland Islands. There is more understanding of this now, and soldier's bodies tend to be repatriated as a matter of course. For those unable to hold a funeral with the body or remains of the deceased, a memorial service is often the key to moving beyond tomorrow.

When someone is simply 'missing', in spite of all the evidence being that they are no longer alive, then many relatives and families refuse to give up hope or have any kind of memorial service. In these terrible circumstances such an action would feel as though it were an acknowledgement that all hope is lost.

Dr Eric Linderman, a Harvard psychiatrist, has said: 'The funeral is psychologically necessary in order to give the opportunity for grief work. The bereaved must be given the capacity to work through his grief if he is to come out of that situation emotionally sound' (Lindemann 1944).

But a funeral or memorial service, although it may be a key element, does not in itself achieve closure. If it did, everyone who was bereaved would be moving forward within weeks of a death.

The death of a child is an ongoing wound, partly due to perceived and potential parental hopes. Every year the loss may be more keenly felt – seeing siblings or friends' children growing up and starting a new life of their own can often bring fresh anguish, making closure seem near impossible.

A child experiencing the death of her or his mother or father is a very sensitive area and it is only relatively recently that the grief of a child has been recognized as being a potentially emotionally damaging life-changing event. Where grief is not recognized and given its due it may take many years before closure is achieved, if indeed it ever is achieved.

I was ten when my mother died. At school, I didn't know whether my teacher and friends had been told – no one ever mentioned it to me and I couldn't bring myself to tell them. So from January to the summer, I pretended that my mother was still alive. Neither my brother nor I attended her funeral. My father had died when I was 18 months old and my step-father gave me no space, time or support to grieve for my mother. I suppose he didn't know how. This had an impact on my entire life, until at 44 I moved to a Greek island. It was here that I became very close to a local woman who had grown up in London and was about the same age as my mother would have been. When she died quite suddenly, the mourning process was entirely different from the one that I witnessed as a child. Her sons owned a bar and immediately after her death her entire family and local friends gathered there, crying openly, talking, hugging and sharing their feelings. It was so open and public and felt so appropriate that the bar was going to be closed for a week. Her death was accompanied by rituals and routines that everyone knew about and observed – and that helped everyone to express their grief.

The funeral was the same day and the body was in an open casket in the church. This was the first time I had seen anyone dead and it removed a lot of fear. Her daughter and sister had washed and dressed her, there was no embalming, she just looked natural and peaceful and the family were sitting right beside the coffin. Everyone held a lighted candle, the priests chanted, people cried openly and at the end of the service several of the men, family and friends, carried the coffin out to the hearse and we all went to the hilltop cemetery overlooking the harbour. The atmosphere was very raw and open – almost chaotic. There was no separation between the process of the burial and the grievers, everyone was part of it and felt part of it.

As the coffin was lowered, my friend's daughter shouted out, 'Have a good journey, mama.' Her voice was raw and so full of emotion. It was disturbing in many ways to be surrounded by so much raw pain, so palpable and open – and yet it felt natural to be so openly dramatic.

I went back to the house with the family and it was then that I cried and her daughters came over and hugged me and, although they lived on a different island and didn't know me very well, they gave me a wonderful feeling of appreciation for how much I loved their mother.

I found this a deeply healing experience, having had no one with whom to share my mother's death. From that time, at ten years old, I felt that I had to grow up, that I was alone, and now at the age of 44 I felt that I had been supported and allowed to grieve so that the circle had in some way finally closed. My husband said afterwards I looked radiant.

The attitude of others

The attitudes of families and friends and others around you can play a major part in allowing or preventing coming to terms with the loss. There are two contradictory attitudes, both damaging and judgemental, which can hamper the natural healing process.

First, 'Are you *still* grieving!?' – a question often unsaid but implied by those around us can leave people feeling both frustrated and inadequate. There is a tendency for others to feel that time should heal, but there is no consensus about how *much* time is needed to achieve healing.

My brother and I were very close – from children we preferred each other's company to that of anyone else. Although we both married and had a family we lived close by and spoke daily and often met up for a drink or a meal. When he had a heart attack and died a part of me died with him. It is perhaps unusual for siblings to be so attached but nevertheless that was the reality.

My husband couldn't understand that two years later there was still a gaping hole in my life and everyone in the family felt it was time I moved on and offered me no comfort at all. I felt very isolated and it caused a rift in my marriage that never really healed.

Everyone's reaction to a significant loss is different and so one bereaved person might find they can get the strength to return to work or to their normal daily routine after a few weeks, whilst another might still feel exhausted and at odds with the world after a year or more. Others, still, might find that they can cope adequately with daily life but a small crisis (a missed bus, a leaking pipe) brings their whole fragile 'coping' edifice tumbling down and they are once more reduced to tears.

Second, conversely, the attitude which implies 'Why *aren't you* still grieving!?' can be a setback. Some of us are happy to share our grief and deeper feelings with the world, others are not. For some people the ultimate embarrassment is to cry in front of others. Even someone who is deeply sad may make an effort not to spoil others' enjoyment of an occasion. This brave effort may be mistaken for lack of feeling. One can sometimes almost hear the unspoken 'Well, she got over it quickly' comment. There are also preconceived notions to contend with:

'She hasn't cried so she can't have taken it in properly.'

'He never speaks of her – how unfeeling.'

'You'd think she would thank me for all the trouble I've gone to. Even grief doesn't excuse bad manners.'

The fact is that some people prefer to cry in private. Some people can only control their feelings by not discussing the subject. Some people are so deeply in shock they do forget their manners – temporarily.

Other problems

Unanswered questions may prevent any ability to move on. Where death has been the result of an accident, those who are mourning may find they are unable to come to terms with the death until after the inquiry into the accident assigns causes or blame. After an accident it may be impossible to achieve closure unless someone is prosecuted and punished for causing the death. Violent death, particularly murder by someone unknown, may prevent those left behind from ever having any feeling of closure.

If the death was preceded by traumatic events in hospital, particularly if mistakes were made – or felt to be made – in treatment leading to death, those who are left may feel that they can only move on by forcing an inquiry and having medical staff responsible called to account. It is important to note, however, that many people in such a situation have stated that they do not want any kind or retribution or revenge but only an acknowledgement that mistakes were made and an apology for what happened. The sad thing is that our present litigious society often prevents the making of a simple apology or the acceptance of blame.

> I remember a girl I worked with who absolutely loved her two dogs. She talked about them frequently and they were a large part of her life. One Monday morning early I got an email from her which simply said 'Dog died – don't be nice to me' and I understood. She felt she could come in to work and carry on normally as long as no one mentioned the dog's death. The reason I understood was because after my father died I found I could talk and behave normally as long as someone else said the words 'her father has died'. As soon as I had to say the words myself the tears would come welling up.

Any unexpected discoveries after death, such as the existence of a hitherto unknown other family, or a mistress, a lover or unexpected debts, can cause such bewilderment and anguish that coming to terms with the death is almost impossible.

> Shortly after my husband's death I received a phone call. The woman gave her name and said she was a friend of my husband. When I said I had not heard him speak of her she replied, 'Perhaps not, but we had a child together.' I had always thought we were happily married, I never dreamed that he had another family. After hearing this news any kind of closure was impossible.

Families in conflict, perhaps contesting the will either in court or in private, will prevent any possibility of closure. This can be an open-ended situation and cause prolonged bad feeling.

My father left the house and estate to my brother and his family. I was devastated by this. I had been the one who had spent the most time with him in his last years and as I was single and lived close by most of his care fell to me. As his will was written in his last year I felt that he had not had the capacity to make this decision, it seemed impossible to me that he would make that kind of decision if he had been able to think it through. The end result was that after several years the will was upheld and my relationship with my brother completely broke down. It was a high price to pay. I can't get over my father's decision and still haven't come to terms with this and it has left me with a feeling of bitterness that prevents me from having any chance of moving forward.

Unresolved issues between the person who died and those left behind can prevent coming to terms with the loss. When the arguments still rage and yet there is no one to respond to them, no one to direct anger towards, closure is a very distant dream. Resolving issues after death is something that can perhaps best be done through professional counselling.

The Mental Capacity Act in the UK has provided a legal framework in which anyone can make their end-of-life wishes known (see *End of Life: The Essential Guide to Caring*, Chapter 1, for more details). Those who take advantage of making an Advance Statement (or a Living Will as it is sometimes known) will not only be giving themselves some peace of mind but will also be helping their relatives and loved ones to avoid the acrimony, stress and guilt which sometimes accompanies the need for others to interpret what the end-of-life wishes might have been. This is a gift which, by relieving the burden of wondering what the person dying would have wanted and thus preventing family conflicts and blame, helps to make healing a possibility.

One of the saddest tales is that of a mother who wasn't told of her son's terminal illness and wasn't given the chance to prepare herself or say goodbye.

My son and his wife moved up to Scotland shortly after they were married and my health made frequent visits very difficult so my husband and I only went to see them once a year. However, for the first year we spoke frequently on the phone, but a few months after our second visit the phone calls became less frequent and my son was often 'abroad' when we called. I was aware that something was not right but when my daughter-in-law called and told us that he had died of cancer I was completely devastated. Why were we not told he was so ill? Why could we not have been given the gift of saying goodbye? My husband died shortly afterwards from cancer, I think it was cancer of the soul. I haven't spoken to my daughter-in-law from that day to this and will never forgive her. Closure is impossible.

The ability to move on and build a life which contains the memory of the person who has died and yet remains happy and fulfilled is perhaps the ideal definition of coming to terms with a loss, but it is not one that everyone is fortunate enough to achieve.

Those who do achieve this may still have days in which they privately revisit their relationship with the person who died with regret or sorrow, triggered perhaps by a memory of a shared joke or piece of music or an anniversary.

It's important to remember that moving beyond tomorrow doesn't mean closing and locking the door on your memories, or on the relationship and love that was shared, but placing this love in one of the rooms of your memory, where it can be visited but yet cannot permeate every 'room' in your life. In this way you can continue to move forward beyond tomorrow whilst living with the memories, and you are not prevented from fully enjoying the present.

Each day after a death may feel like a challenge, but by focusing more on today and less on yesterday you will make progress. Remember that recovery after bereavement is not a steady progression. There will be bad days and good days.

The journey beyond tomorrow is not an easy one – but we hope with the aid of this book to have shown you a path that will take you there.

Bibliography

Bor, R., Miller, R., Goldman, E. and Scher, I. (1993) 'The meaning of bad news in HIV disease: counselling about dreaded issues revisited.' *Counselling Psychology Quarterly 6*, 69–80.

Brolin, S.E. (1987) 'The effects of companion animals during conjugal bereavement.' *Anthrozoos 1*, 21, 26–35.

Buckman, R. (1992) *How to Break Bad News: A Guide for Health Professionals.* Baltimore, MD: John Hopkins University Press.

Corporation for National and Community Service, Office of Research and Policy Development (2007) *The Health Benefits of Volunteering: A Review of Recent Research.* Washington, DC: Office of Research and Policy Development.

Fearnley, R. (2012) *Communicating with Children when a Parent is at the End of Life.* London: Jessica Kingsley Publishers.

George, H. (1997) 'Spiritual Beliefs and the Dying Process: A Report on a National Survey'. Available at www.ncf.org/ reports/rpt_fetzer_contents.html.

Goer, G. (1967) *Death, Grief, and Mourning.* New York: Doubleday Anchor.

Hardiman, D. (2010) 'Companion Animals in the Family.' *The SCAS Journal XXII*, 4, 14–17.

Jordan, M., and Kauffmann, J.C. (2010) *End of Life: The Essential Guide to Caring.* London: Hammersmith Press (www.endoflifebook.com).

Klass, D., Silverman, P.R. and Nickman, S.L. (eds) (1996) *Continuing Bonds: New Understandings of Grief.* Washington, DC: Taylor and Francis.

Kübler-Ross, E. (1969) *On Death and Dying.* New York: Simon & Schuster.

Lindemann, E. (1944) 'Symptomatology and Management of Acute Grief.' *American Journal of Psychiatry 151*, 6, 155–160.

McGraw, P. (2008) *Real Life: Preparing for the 7 Most Challenging Days of Your Life.* New York: Free Press.

McNicholas, J., Gilby, A., Rennie, A., Ahmed, S., Dono, J. and Ormerod, E. (2005) 'Pet ownership and human health: a brief review of evidence and issues.' *British Medical Journal 331*, 7527, 1252–1254.

Silverman, P.R. (1999) *Never Too Young to Know: Death in Children's Lives.* Oxford: Oxford University Press.

Temes, R. (1992) *Living with an empty chair: a guide through grief.* New Jersey: New Horizons Press.

Tuffrey-Wijne, I. (2012) *How to Break Bad News to People with Intellectual Disabilities.* London: Jessica Kingsley Publishers.

Worden, W. J. (2009) *Grief Counseling and Grief Therapy, Fourth Edition: A Handbook for the Mental Health Practitioner.* New York: Springer Publishing Company.

Zisook, S. (1987) *Biopsychosocial Aspects of Bereavement (Progress in Psychiatry).* Arlington, Virginia: American Psychiatric Publishing.

Zisook, S. and Shuchter S.R. (1993) 'Uncomplicated Bereavement.' *Journal of Clinical Psychiatry 54*, 10, 365–372.

Resources

UK
Grief and Bereavement
www.cruse.org.uk
Cruse Bereavement Care promotes the wellbeing of bereaved people and enables anyone bereaved by death to understand their grief and cope with their loss. The national telephone helpline is 0844 477 9400.

www.compassionatefriends.org/home.aspx
Whether your family has had a child die (at any age from any cause) or you are trying to help those who have gone through this life altering experience, The Compassionate Friends exists to provide friendship, understanding, and hope to those going through the natural grieving process.

http://hospicenet.org/html/knowledge.html
For patients and families facing life-threatening illness.

www.samaritans.org
People talk to Samaritans anytime they like, in their own way, and off the record - about whatever's getting to them. They do not have to be suicidal.
Telephone: 08457 90 90 90 (UK)
1850 60 90 90 (ROI)

www.cinnamon.org.uk
The Cinnamon Trust is the national charity for the elderly, the terminally ill and their pets.

Vehicle Licensing, Passports and Tax
DVLA:
www.dft.gov.uk/dvla
The Driver and Vehicle Licensing Agency (DVLA), previously the Driver and Vehicle Licensing Centre (DVLC).

Passport Office:
www.direct.gov.uk/prod_consum_dg/groups/dg_digitalassets/@dg/@en/documents/digitalasset/dg_188463.pdf

What to do with a passport when the passport holder has died:
www.homeoffice.gov.uk/agencies-public-bodies/ips
The Identity and Passport Service is responsible for issuing UK passports and for administering the civil registration process in England and Wales. It is an executive agency of the Home Office.

www.hmrc.gov.uk/sa/rec-needed.htm
If you are the personal representative of someone who has died, you will need to settle their tax affairs up to the date they died.

www.deceasedpreferenceservice.co.uk
Registering with The Deceased Preference Service is one of the quickest and easiest ways to ensure unwanted mail addressed to the deceased is stopped. It also ensures that the risk of identity theft is reduced giving double peace of mind.

Support
Stroke Association:
www.stroke.org.uk
The Stroke Association is the major stroke charity in the UK.
Telephone: 0303 3033 100

Alzheimer's Society:
www.alzheimers.org.uk
The Alzheimer's Society National Dementia Helpline can provide information, support, guidance and signposting to other appropriate organizations.
Telephone: 0300 222 1122.

Cancer Support:
www.macmillan.org.uk/Aboutus/AboutUsHome.aspx
If you have been diagnosed with cancer, or a loved one has, you will want a team of people in your corner supporting you every step of the way. Macmillan Cancer Support provides practical, medical and financial support and pushes for better cancer care.
Telephone: 020 7840 7840
Address:
Macmillan Cancer Support
89 Albert Embankment
London
SE1 7UQ

Child Bereavement Support:

www.childbereavement.org.uk/For/ForProfessionals/BestPracticeGuidance AdditionalInfo

Child Bereavement UK believes that all families should have access to the support and information they need when a child grieves or when a child dies. Through understanding their grieving process and receiving help in dealing with bereavement from appropriately trained professionals, families can learn to live with their grief and begin rebuilding their lives.

Memorials

www.digitaljewellery.com

www.eternitycrystal.com

www.heavensabovefireworks.com

www.lifeforalife.org.uk

www.muchloved.com/g_home.aspx

www.phoenix-diamonds.com

www.rememberacharity.org.uk

www.rhs.org.uk

www.sentiment-productions.co.uk

Personal Effects

www.amazon.co.uk

www.bookaid.org

www.bookharvest.co.uk

www.disabledgear.com

www.ebay.co.uk

www.gov.uk/after-a-death/overview

www.gumtree.com

www.snaffleup.co.uk

www.uk.freecycle.org

USA
Grief and Bereavement
www.samaritansusa.org
Samaritans USA, the organization comprising the individual Samaritans centres operating in the United States, is a member of the world's oldest and largest suicide prevention network, with 400 centres in 38 countries.

www.griefshare.org
GriefShare is a friendly, caring group of people who will walk alongside you through one of life's most difficult experiences. You don't have to go through the grieving process alone.
Telephone: 800 395 5755
International: 919 562 2112
Email: info@griefshare.org

www.compassionatefriends.org/home.aspx
'The Compassionate Friends is about transforming the pain of grief into the elixir of hope. It takes people out of the isolation society imposes on the bereaved and lets them express their grief naturally. With the shedding of tears, healing comes. And the newly bereaved get to see people who have survived and are learning to live and love again' (Simon Stephens, founder of The Compassionate Friends).
Telephone: 630 990 0010
Toll-Free: 877 969 0010

www.bereavedparentsusa.org
Bereaved Parents USA is a national non-profit self-help group that offers support, understanding, compassion and hope especially to the newly bereaved, be they bereaved parents, grandparents or siblings struggling to rebuild their lives after the death of their children, grandchildren or siblings.
Address:
National Office
PO Box 622
St Peters MO 63376

Vehicle Licensing, Passports and Tax
Vehicle Licensing USA:
www.onlinedmv.com
www.usa.gov/Topics/Motor-Vehicles.shtml

USA Passport Cancellation:
Mail the passport of a deceased relative for cancellation. Send it to the Consular Lost and Stolen Passport (CLASP) unit of Passport Services. The address is: Attention CLASP, 1111 19th St. N.W., Suite 500, Washington,

D.C. 20036. Include a copy of your relative's death certificate and a letter requesting cancellation of the passport.

USA Tax Office:
www.irs.gov/uac/Form-W-2,-Wage-and-Tax-Statement
www.irs.gov

Support

USA Stroke Association:
www.strokeassociation.org/STROKEORG

Cancer Support Groups USA:
www.aacr.org/home/survivors--advocates/information-about-support-groups,-clinical-trials,-financial-help-and-fundraising/how-to-find-a-support-group.aspx

USA Alzheimer's Support:
www.alz.org

Horticulture

www.ahs.org
The American Horticultural Society is one of the oldest national gardening organizations in the country. Since 1922, it has been a trusted source of high quality gardening and horticultural information.
Main telephone number: 703 768 5700
Main fax: 703 768 8700
Publications fax: 703 768 7533

Memorials

www.monumentbuilders.org/builders_certified_memorialist_program.php
Monument Builders of North America is a trade association that is over 100 years old.

www.huffingtonpost.ca/2012/05/25/ash-scattering_n_1545627.html
Ash Scattering: Not-Traditonal Ways to Be Memorialized is an article written by Rebecca Zamon.

www.celestis.com/default.asp
Telephone: 1 866. 7 Rocket (1 866 776 2538) or +1 713 524 2568
Fax: +1 713 527 7149
Address:
2536 Amherst St. Ste. J
Houston Texas 77005, U.S.A.

Personal Effects

www.pva.org/site/c.ajIRK9NJLcJ2E/b.8010313/k.5D02/National_Thrift_Program.htm

Paralysed Veterans of America's nationwide thrift programme helps support severely injured veterans and their families. Through the donations of new and gently used clothing and household items, they are able to serve local communities and empower veterans to heal and lead successful lives. All donations are tax deductible and residential pickup is free of charge. Telephone numbers are local and listed.

www.use.salvationarmy.org

With your help, The Salvation Army will continue assisting those who are homeless, abused or disadvantaged.

www.donationtown.org

DonationTown.org offers the best listing of charities that will come to your home and pick up your donations. For free. All of the non-profit charities on Donation Town offer an IRS tax deduction receipt whenever you donate. Donate to the charity of your choice!

www.freecycle.org/group/US

Freecycle currently keeps 500 tons a day out of landfills. By giving freely with no strings attached people from all walks of life have joined to turn trash into treasure.

http://gumtreeads.com/classifieds

GumtreeAds is a large network of online classifieds and community websites. Classified ads can either be free or paid depending on the product category and the market niche.

www.ebay.com

Ebay Inc. (stlyised as ebay) is an American multinational internet consumer-to-consumer corportation, headquartered in San Jose, California.

www.craigslist.org/about/sites

Local classifieds and forums – community moderated and largely free. Links to different areas in the United States are available on the site.

www.harvestbooks.com

Harvest Book Company is a large buyer of used and rare books. Through its donation programmes, it supports several local non-profits, including many local public libraries.
Telephone: 1 800 563 1222

www.dotmed.com

DOTmed.com is the world's leading public platform for buying and selling medical equipment, parts and services. It welcomes more than 20,000 unique visitors every day. DOTmed was founded in 1999 as an open marketplace for healthcare professionals, medical equipment manufacturers, brokers and dealers, and today has more than 200,000 registered users.

Volunteering

www.ehow.com/how_8697370_volunteer-feed-homeless.html
Hunger is an issue commonly associated with homelessness. For those living on the streets, finding food can be a daily struggle.

www.salvationarmyusa.org/usn/www_usn_2.nsf/vw-dynamic-arrays/89941F85D 7A2ECAC802573250030C4F0?openDocument&charset=utf-8
Almost 3,400,000 individuals of all ages volunteered their time, talents, and resources to assist The Salvation Army's work

www.volunteermatch.org
VolunteerMatch strengthens communities by making it easier for good people and good causes to connect.
Main Office:
Telephone: (415) 241 6868
Fax: (415) 241 6869
Address:
VolunteerMatch
550 Montgomery Street, 8th Floor
San Francisco
CA 94111

Canada
Grief and Bereavement

www.befrienders.org/helplines/helplines.asp?c2=Canada
The main aim of the centres is to give emotional support to people when they are suicidal. The centres also alleviate misery, loneliness, despair and depression by listening to anyone who feels they have nowhere else to turn. The people who run the centres – befrienders – are volunteers who have all been specially trained. The work is non-political and non-religious.

www.suicidepreventionhelp.com/directory/Crisis_Centers/North_America/Canada
This suicide prevention website offers a Friendship Letter for those who are despairing and thinking about suicide, and also for people who are concerned that a loved one may be suicidal.

Vehicle Licensing, Passports and Tax
Vehicle Licensing:
www.mto.gov.on.ca/english/dandv
Telephone: 416 326 1234
Toll-free: 1 800 267 9097

Passports:
Cancelling Passports:

www.passeport.gc.ca/support/faq.aspx?lang=eng&id=q550

Include a copy of the death certificate and a letter indicating whether the cancelled passport should be destroyed or returned to you. The passport should be sent by mail to the following address:

Passport Canada
Foreign Affairs and International Trade Canada
Gatineau
QC K1A 0G3

Canadian tax office:

www.cra-arc.gc.ca/cntct/tso-bsf-eng.html

You can get the address and fax number of a tax services office or tax centre by selecting your province or territory of residence.

Support

Stroke Support:

www.canadianstrokenetwork.ca

The Canadian Stroke Network's mission is to reduce the impact of stroke on Canadians through collaborations that create valuable new knowledge in stroke.

Address:
Canadian Stroke Network
600 Peter Morand Crescent, Suite 301
Ottawa, ON
K1G 5Z3

Cancer Support:

www.cancer.ca/ontario.aspx

Thanks to the generosity of its donors and to the work of its volunteers and staff, the Canadian Cancer Society is leading the way in the fight against cancer.

Telephone: (416) 488 5400 or (416) 488 5400
Toll-free: 1 800 268 8874 or 1 800 268 8874
email: webmaster@ontario.cancer.ca
Address:
Canadian Cancer Society
Ontario Division
55 St. Clair Avenue West, Suite 500
Toronto, ON M4V 2Y7

Alzheimer's Society of Canada:
www.alzheimer.ca/en
The Alzheimer's Society is Canada's leading health charity for people living with Alzheimer's disease and other dementias.
Telephone: 1 800-616 8816
email: info@alzheimer.ca

Canadian Dementia Action Network (CDAN):
www.alzheimer.ca/en
Dedicated to eradicating Alzheimer's disease and related dementias (ADRD). CDAN brings together Canada's world-class biomedical researchers and clinicians for the purpose of quickly identifying promising treatments for ADRD.
Telephone: 1 604 822 7377
email: admin@cdan.ca

Memorials

www.omba.com/main.php
An association of monument manufacturers and builders established to promote the monument industry and to create and maintain a high standard of business ethics for its members to follow.

www.jewelrykeepsakes.com/Cermation-Jewelry-Canada-s/342.htm
Telephone: 1 887 723 7229

www.pacificurns.com
Telephone: 1 888 832 1195

www.ajourneywithwings.com/about
This is a business dedicated to scattering cremated remains by aeroplane. It provides a personalized farewell with locations and participation options that are as unique as the life of the deceased.
Telephone: 1 562 691 7227

www.huggableurns.com
Telephone: 1 530 351 1416

www.cremationsolutions.com/Crystals-from-Ashes-c97.html
Cremation Crystals are cremation jewellery keepsakes and pet memorials that infuse your loved ones' ashes into a crystal glass memorial.
Telephone: 1 877 365 9474

www.neptunesociety.com/memorial-reef
In addition to providing a permanent legacy for those who loved the ocean, the Neptune Memorial Reef™ is attracting recreational scuba divers, marine biologists, students, researchers and ecologists from all over the world. The Reef is free and accessible to all visitors.
Telephone: 1 888 637 8863

Horticultural

www.gardenontario.org

The Ontario Horticultural Association is a volunteer, charitable organization whose mission is to provide leadership and assist in the promotion of education and interest in all areas of horticulture and related environmental issues in Ontario, through an expanding network of horticultural societies dedicated to the beautification of their communities

www.cshs.ca

The Canadian Society for Horticultural Science (CSHS) was founded in 1956. The membership is divided into five regional sections: Atlantic, Quebec, Ontario, Prairie and Pacific. CSHS members (scientists, educators, students, extension agents and industry personnel) are involved in and make significant advances in research, teaching, information and technology related to all horticultural crops: fruits, vegetables, nuts, herbs, greenhouse, flowers, nursery plants and more. There are many advantage to becoming a CSHS member.

www.salvationarmy.ca/volunteer

Telephone: 1 800 725 2769
Address:
The Salvation Army
Territorial Headquarters for Canada and Bermuda
2 Overlea Boulevard
Toronto, Ontario M4H 1P4

http://volunteer.ca

Volunteer Canada works with over 200 volunteer centres nationwide. Volunteer Canada boasts a membership of over 1,200 groups.
Telephone: (613) 231 4371 or 1 (800) 670 0401
email: info@volunteer.ca
Address:
UnderOneRoof
251 Bank Street, 5th Floor
Ottawa, ON K2N 1X3

Australia

Grief and Bereavement

www.befrienders.org/helplines/helplines.asp?c2=Australia

The main aim of the centres is to give emotional support to people when they are suicidal. The centres also alleviate misery, loneliness, despair and depression by listening to anyone who feels they have nowhere else to turn. Telephone numbers of the different Befriender helplines listed according to state are on their website.

Vehicle Licensing, Passports and Tax

Register for an australia.gov.au account to access Australian Government online services from one central place.

http://australia.gov.au/topics/transport/registration-and-licences
Find out how to obtain, renew or transfer a vehicle licence in Western Australia, including repairable, written-off and hail-damaged vehicles.

www.transport.wa.gov.au/licensing/20410.asp
Driver and Vehicle Services.
Telephone: 131 156 (for all licensing and motor vehicle queries.)

Australian Passport Office:
www.passports.gov.au/Web/index.aspx
Telephone: 131 232
8am−8pm Mon−Fri
8:30am−5pm weekends and most public holidays.
Address:
GPO Box 4708
Sydney NSW 2001

Australian Tax Office:
www.ato.gov.au
Telephone numbers are listed according to tax enquiry

Support

Stroke Support:
http://strokefoundation.com.au
The National Stroke Foundation is a national not-for-profit organization that works with stroke survivors, carers, health professionals, government and the public to reduce the impact of stroke on the Australian community.
Telephone: 1800 787 653

Cancer Support:
www.cancer.org.au
Cancer Council Australia and its members undertake a broad range of activities.

Cancer Council Helpline:
Telephone: 13 11 20

National Dementia Helpline:
www.fightdementia.org.au/contact-us.aspx
Telephone: 1800 100 500
This helpline operates during business hours and provides information, support and referral services for health professionals, people with dementia, their carers and families.

Alzheimer's Association Dementia Helpline:
Telephone: 1800 639 331

Horticultural

www.horticulture.com.au
Horticulture Australia Limited (HAL) is a not-for-profit, industry-owned company. It works in partnership with Australia's horticulture industries to invest in research, development and marketing programmes that provide benefit to industry and the wider community.

www.daff.gov.au/agriculture-food/food/publications/hort-fact-sheet
Australia's horticulture industry has long enjoyed a domestic and international reputation for quality - primarily due to its high standards across all stages of the supply chain, from farm to consumer.

Memorials

www.health.vic.gov.au/cemeteries/medical_prac/stonemasons.htm
The department does not deal with the direct regulation of stonemasons. However, the *Cemeteries and Crematoria Act 2003* regulates the work that can be conducted by stonemasons regarding the establishment and alteration of memorials and places of interment. Importantly, under section 99 of the Act, a cemetery trust must approve all applications to establish or alter a memorial or place of interment.
Freephone: 1800 034 280

www.budgetlife.com/blog/weird-cremations
As cremations have become more and more popular in recent years, people have devised a number of unusual ways to commemorate the dearly departed. If you're looking for a unique way to be remembered, this site lists 12 strange things you can do with cremated remains.

PERSONAL EFFECTS

www.u3aonline.org.au/u3a/find
University of the Third Age (U3A). U3A Online is the world's first virtual University of the Third Age delivering online learning via the internet.

www.bookmonkey.com.au
Australia's website for buying selling and exchanging second-hand books.

http://geo.craigslist.org/iso/au
Local classifieds and forums — community moderated, and largely free. Links to different areas in Australia available on the site.

GRIEF SUPPORT SERVICES

www.grief.org.au

The Australian Centre for Grief and Bereavement is a not-for-profit organization established to provide a range of education, counselling, research and clinical services for those working in and affected by experiences of grief and bereavement.

http://grieflink.org.au/?page_id=18

Bereavement Information and Referral Service.
Telephone: 1300 664 786

VOLUNTEERING

www.govolunteer.com.au/Opportunity/SearchResults

GoVolunteer has a large range of volunteer roles including one-off, short-term and long-term opportunities and many volunteering organizations can be flexible with times. It makes it easy for you to find a volunteer role that suits your interests, motivation, availability and location.

www.vinnies.org.au/homeless-services-national?link=452

The care of homeless youth, women, men and families is a primary concern of the St Vincent de Paul Society. It currently funds homeless men's hostels, women's refuges, homeless family services, youth crisis centres, youth drop-in centres, drug and alcohol rehabilitation centres and 'night patrol' or 'soup van' services.

Index